Dazzle

Dazzle

CREATING ARTISTIC JEWELRY & DISTINCTIVE ACCESSORIES

LINDA FRY KENZLE

Chilton Book Company
Radnor, Pennsylvania

Published in Radnor, Pennsylvania 19089, by Chilton Book Company

Photography by Nick Novelli

Book designed by Anthony Jacobson

Additional copies of this book may be ordered from any bookstore, or directly through Chilton Book Company (1-800-274-7066).

Manufactured in the United States of America

Library of Congress Cataloging in Publication Data
Kenzle, Linda Fry.
Dazzle : creating artistic jewelry & distinctive accessories/ by Linda Fry Kenzle.
p. cm.—(StarWear)
Includes index.
ISBN 0-8019-8638-9 (pbk.)
1. Jewelry making. 2. Dress accessories. I. Title. II. Series.
TT212.K46 1995 95-7315
745.594'2—dc20 CIP

1 2 3 4 5 6 7 8 9 0 4 3 2 1 0 9 8 7 6 5

To my mother

Ione

who inspired and encouraged

my love for jewelry

by always

wearing

dazzling pieces

every day

CONTENTS

FOREWORD

I first learned Linda's name in the '80s when I subscribed to her *Stylepages* and saw her work in exhibits. Linda's wearable art was immediately recognizable—it had a creative twist and gave the feeling she had fun designing it. She's still having fun creating: *Embellishments* was her first Chilton book, and now she shares her knowledge of making jewelry and accessories in *Dazzle*.

If you love wearing original jewelry and accessories, but gasp at the cost, your worries are over. Linda shows how to do-it-yourself inexpensively—with everything from traditional fiber, leather, wood, and paper, to man-made polymer clay and Friendly Plastic. She works with beads and buttons, too, finding them in her stash or at garage sales and flea markets—it's part of the fun.

Dazzle is a book of techniques to learn and projects to try. It's also a reference book of paint brush styles, bead sizes and shapes, and supplies you need: what they look like, and how to use them.

Whether you prefer using a needle or glue, paint or dye, hand-sewing or sewing machine, here are over 30 dazzling ideas for you to create—so let's get started!

Jackie Dodson

ACKNOWLEDGMENTS

Thanks to the following family, friends, and colleagues who have been generous with their time, encouragement, and expertise: Don Carlo, Joshua Clay, Jeremiah Kenzle, T.C. Kenzle, Cendra Eastlake, Lily West, Susan Clarey, Robbie Fanning, Susan Keller, Barbara Ellis, Bruce McKenzie, Tony Jacobson, Nick Novelli, Freya Ellinwood, Debra Gust, Myrna Kanter, Bette M. Kelley, Roberta Z. Marco, Maxine Peretz Prange, and Jackie Dodson.

The author gratefully acknowledges the support of: American & Efird, Inc., The Bead Shop, Communication Concepts, Delta Technical Coatings, Decart, Inc., June Tailor, Inc., Loew-Cornell, Palmer Paint Products, Inc., Polyform Products Co., Rupert, Gibbon & Spider, Savoir-Faire, Snafail Co., Inc.

INTRODUCTION

Small details can make a resounding impact—especially in creating your own personal style. A one-of-a-kind art pin fastened to the lapel of your suit creates a signature statement. The addition of a gorgeous silk scarf tossed casually about the neck adds a sense of drama. A simple baseball-style cap made up in hand-dyed cottons, and embellished with cloth roses sends the message of your playful quality, your delightful sense of humor. A striking polymer clay neckpiece can enliven any outfit and make it sing.

Accessories are the key to transformation. With a basic solid-colored wardrobe done in classic lines, you can achieve a pleasantly varied look with the addition of a few distinctive elements. One day add the Peacock Feather Belt and the hand-beaded Ebony Triangle Pin; the next, use the hand-felted Boater, Memory Wrap Bracelet, and the Thistle Cutwork Bag. Assemble an exotic look with the Ethnic Mirrored Pendant and leather Flap Bag with Shell Medallion. For a very contemporary look toss on a hand-painted silk scarf with the ultramodern Watercolor & Jewel Earrings.

Use plain clothing as a canvas on which to play out the presentation of artistic jewelry and distinctive accessories. The new solid-colored dressing systems are ideal. Donna Karan's Essentials and Randolph Duke's Five Easy Pieces are complete mini-wardrobes. Norma Kamali also has a new line, and pattern companies offer all-in-one patterns to make your own matching clothing collections.

If you are strapped by a shortage of finances, handmade jewelry and accessories can bring a freshness to your wardrobe without making a hole in your pocket. A bit of this, a little of that (beads, cloth, and findings you may already have on hand) can be worked up into an eye-popping adornment. I love what Julian Robinson wrote in *Fashion in the 40's:* "a hat is a cosmetic, a beautifier, giving uplift to tired face lines that are down-bent. A hat softens your profile, broadens your brow, balances a weak chin, helps a poor feature and plays up a good one. A hat can lie like a trooper about your age and it can be the one bit of nonsense in your new utility wardrobe." Wow! the power of accessories!

In this book, I've included a wide variety of styles to give you a nice range of options. Although the book is based on projects, each project uses different techniques. The explanations are meant to employ many different styles of creating so you can be your own designer once you've completed the projects in this book. You'll find both ultramodern designs and romantic, antique inspirations crafted from materials used long ago. I've also added a selection of ethnic-based fabrications celebrating the spirit of other countries of the world. Select those that appeal to you. Hopefully a few of the designs will tickle you to try something new, to add diversity to your style.

I have also added a mini-gallery of interesting jewelry and accessory work being done by artists from across the country. I include them to inspire you. Look at these special pieces as you would in a gallery setting. Notice the way these artists handle form, line, shape, texture, and color. Please do not literally copy these pieces. They are the signature work of each artist represented. Rather I hope their work will encourage you to create pieces of the same quality.

Time is precious and fleeting. Indeed we all try to accomplish a great deal in every 24 hours we are given. To that end I have included some particularly time-saving projects. Look for the star symbol (left) when you want to create dazzle but time is at a premium.

The color elements shown here are my selections. I urge you to create fabulous pieces of jewelry and sensational accessories to emphasize and express your personal style.

Change colors, make unique material choices, use different motifs, use different threads, beads...show off your creative prowess. Create your own personal adornments.

L.F.K.

She no longer painted, but collected textiles, paintings and jewelry. She spent her entire morning getting dressed. She no longer sat before an easel, but before a dressing table, and made an art of dressing in native textiles and jewels.

When she finally descended the staircase in the hotel, she became an animated painting. Everyone's eyes were drawn to her. All the colors of Diego Rivera and Orozco were draped on her body. Sometimes her dress seemed painted with large brushstrokes, sometimes roughly dyed like the costumes of the poor. Other times she wore what looked like fragments of ancient Mayan murals, bold symmetrical designs in charcoal outlines with the colors dissolved by age. Heavy earrings of Aztec warriors, necklaces and bracelets of shell, gold and silver medallions and carved head and amulets, animal and bones, all these caught the light as she moved.

It was her extreme liveliness that may have prevented her from working upon a painting, and turned a passion for color and textures upon her own body.

Anais Nin
Seduction of the Minotaur

KOREA

PART ONE

JEWELRY

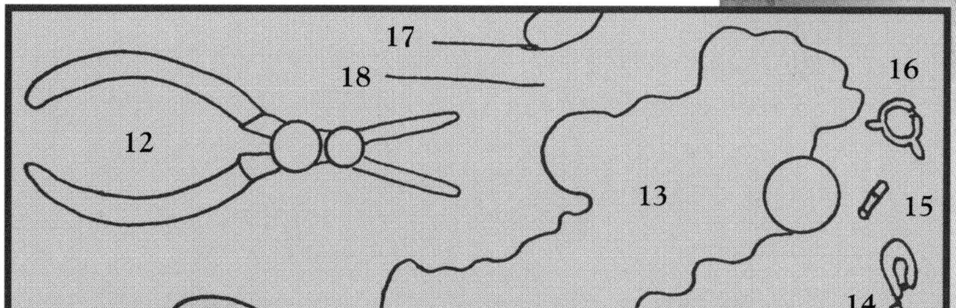

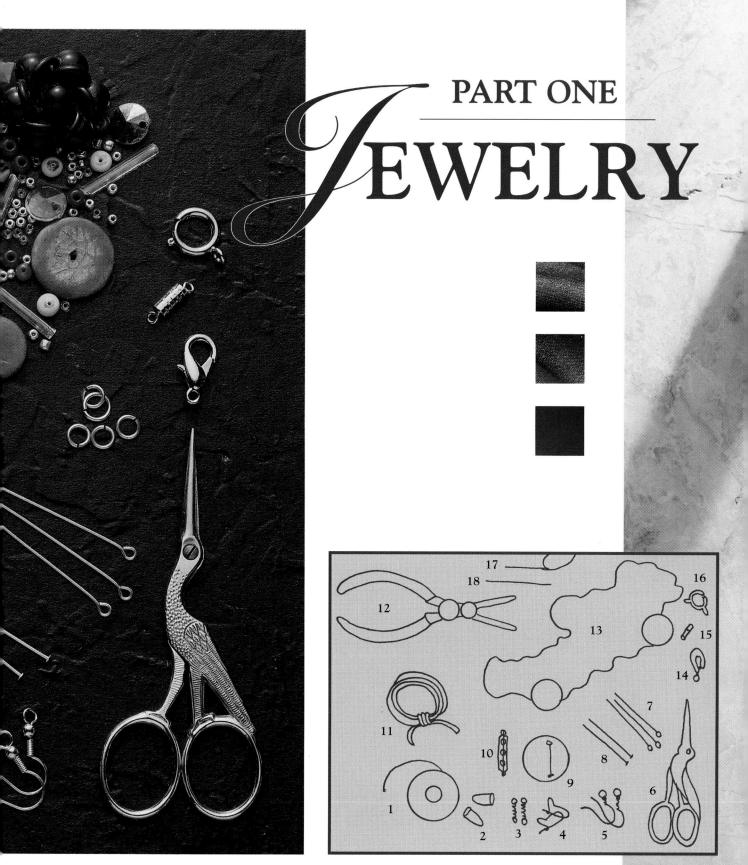

1. *Tiger tail* **2.** *End cones* **3.** *Coil ends* **4.** *Kidney ear wires* **5.** *French ear wires* **6.** *Stork embroidery scissors* **7.** *Eye pins* **8.** *Head pins* **9.** *Circle pin back* **10.** *Standard pin back* **11.** *Leather cord* **12.** *Jewelry pliers/wire cutters* **13.** *Beads, buttons, shells* **14.** *Lobster claw clasp* **15.** *Barrel clasp* **16.** *Spring ring clasp* **17.** *Quilting needle* **18.** *Beading needle*

CHAPTER 1

JEWELRYMAKING ESSENTIALS

Tools of the Trade

Jewelrymaking by hand is a very seductive process. With just a few simple tools and a cache of beautiful beads you can create distinctive, mouthwatering pieces that add sparkle and fantasy to your wardrobe. And that's just the beginning. Why not try making your own earrings out of plastic? A colorful pin out of polymer clay? A stylish bracelet with antique buttons? An exotic pendant out of velvet, mirrors, and embroidery? Jewelry made of paper, wood, shells. . . . The possibilities are endless. You'll find descriptions of all of these materials and projects—and more—in the following pages.

In this first section, devoted to the basics of jewelry-making, we'll explore the tools and materials ("findings") used to create striking jewelry. You'll learn how to use these findings, as well as the lingo of beading. I'll give you lots of information so that once you've mastered the techniques, you can go on to design your own pieces that reflect your personal style.

Let's look at the materials first. Then we'll jump right into the projects.

Beads

Beads are magical. Tiny seed beads flicker with fire. Crystal beads throw off rainbows of colored light. Transparent Venetian glass beads reveal intense color often accented with golden swirls and glass bead droplets.

Beads are tiny masterpieces to be admired singly or in combination with plainer, solid-colored beads, which form a frame of sorts to play up their striking magnificence.

All beads are wonderful, whether they are made of glass, wood, polymer clay, plastic, or paper. Most beadworkers prefer

SEED BEADS PER INCH

Use the following counts of seed beads per inch to plan your own designs. (Please note that these are approximations.)

Bead Size	Beads Per Inch
11	20
8	12
5	7

Bead Sizes in Millimeters

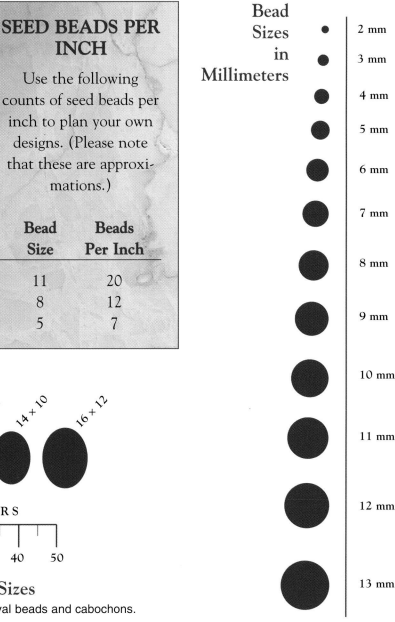

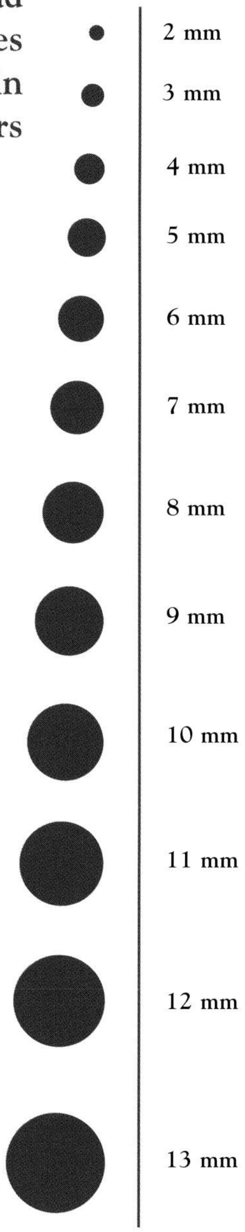

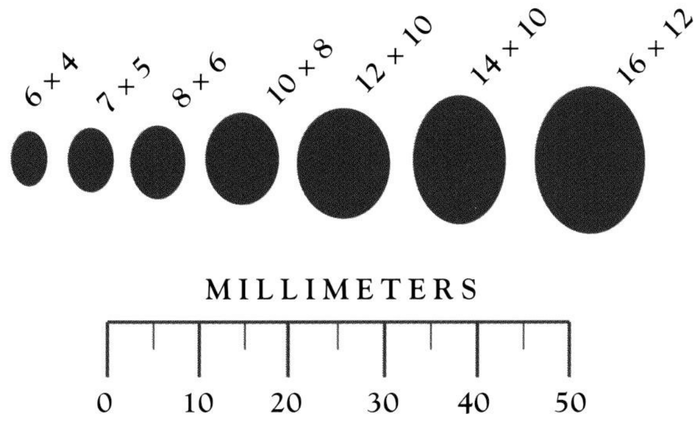

Oval Bead Sizes

Use this handy guide to measure oval beads and cabochons.

Bead Shapes

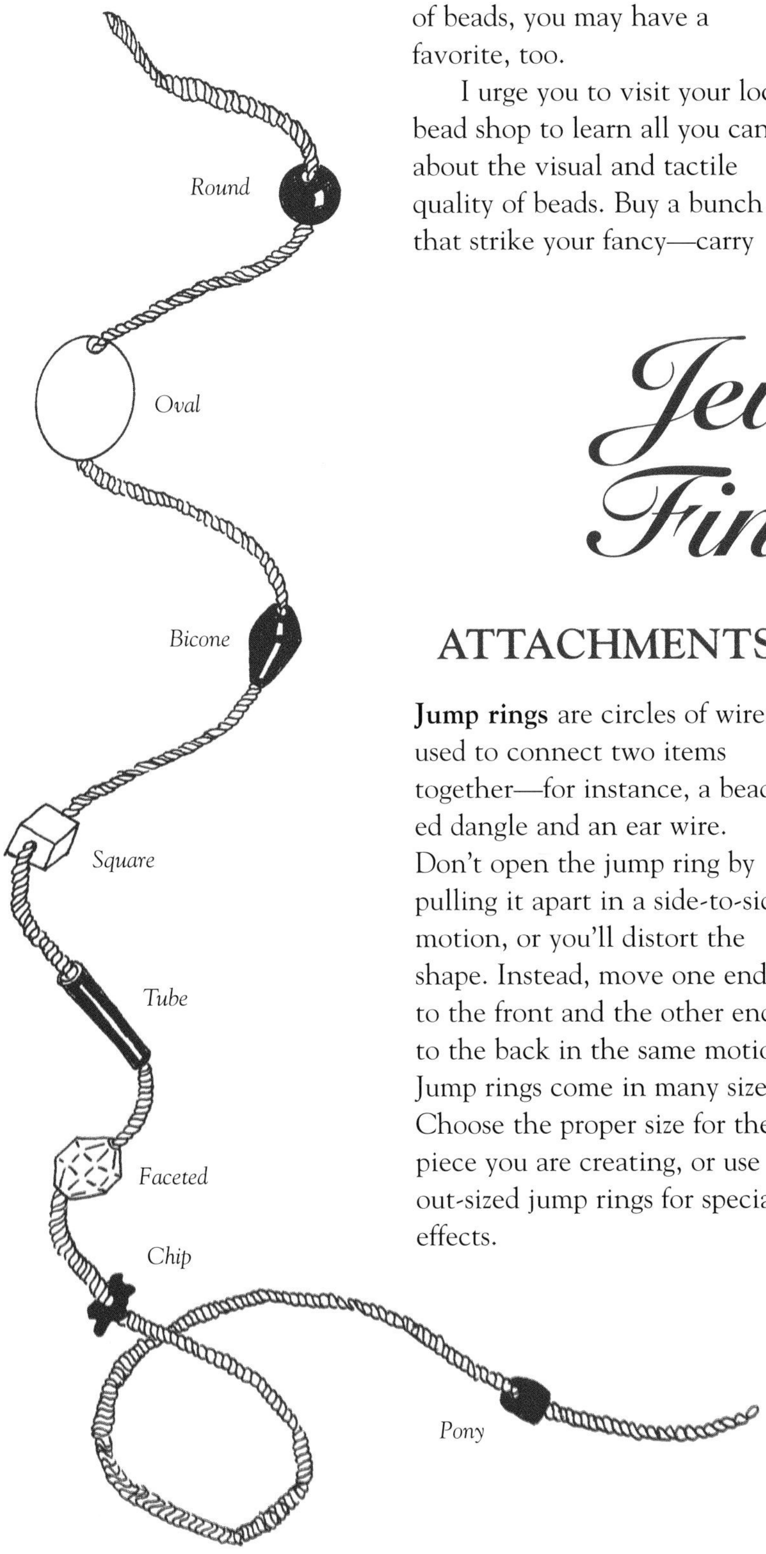

one type of bead to all others. Once you've become acquainted with all the different kinds of beads, you may have a favorite, too.

I urge you to visit your local bead shop to learn all you can about the visual and tactile quality of beads. Buy a bunch that strike your fancy—carry them around in a velvet pouch, roll them in your fingers, hold them up to the sun to expose their inner beauty. Go to bead shows, visit galleries, order catalogs, subscribe to periodicals. Probe the possibilities. You'll find a special Resources section at the back of the book to help get you started.

Jewelry Findings

ATTACHMENTS

Jump rings are circles of wire used to connect two items together—for instance, a beaded dangle and an ear wire. Don't open the jump ring by pulling it apart in a side-to-side motion, or you'll distort the shape. Instead, move one end to the front and the other end to the back in the same motion. Jump rings come in many sizes. Choose the proper size for the piece you are creating, or use out-sized jump rings for special effects.

Jump ring

Eye pins and head pins are pieces of wire that come in various lengths. The longer 3-inch pins are the most useful, since they can be cut to size. The eye

Eye pin *Head pin*

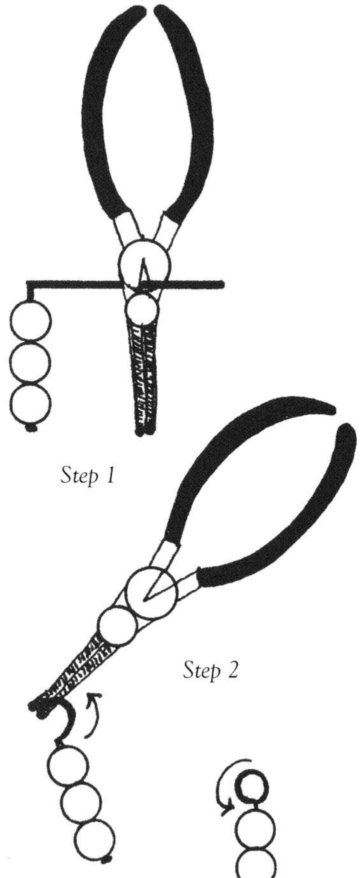

Step 1

Step 2

Step 3

pin has a loop ending and is usually used in the middle of a design—for example, to attach a length of beads in the middle of a dangle. The head pin has a flat end, like that of a flat-head nail. It is used as a finishing piece at the end of a dangle.

To attach an eye pin or a head pin to an ear wire or other finding, follow these three steps: 1) Bend the pin to form a right angle and clip off any excess wire over ¾ inch. 2) Using needle-nose pliers, grab the end of the wire and turn it in a spiral motion halfway into a loop. 3) Grab the wire end once again and turn the pliers until the end meets the wire to form a loop. Once you have mastered this technique, you can create the loop in two steps rather than three.

STANDARD JEWELRY LENGTHS

Listed are the usual jewelry lengths, but in actuality a bracelet, for instance, can measure anywhere from 6 inches to 8 inches. For a custom fit measure your wrist and add 1 inch for wearing ease. For a custom necklace length, cut a piece of cord to the desired length and place it around your neck. Adjust the size as necessary to attain the look you desire.

7" — bracelet
14" — dog collar
16" — choker
18" — princess
24" — matinee
32" — opera
36" — rope
48" — lasso

CLASPS

Spring ring clasps are the most common type of clasp used on costume jewelry as well as fine metal jewelry. They range in size from 6mm to 12mm or larger. Attach the spring ring clasp (or any other clasp) using a jump ring. Add another jump ring at the other end of the piece of jewelry to receive the clasp.

Spring ring clasp

Lobster claw clasps are shaped somewhat like the claws of a lobster. More substantial in weight than spring ring clasps, they look good on jewelry made of heavier materials. Their contemporary styling gives them an uptown look.

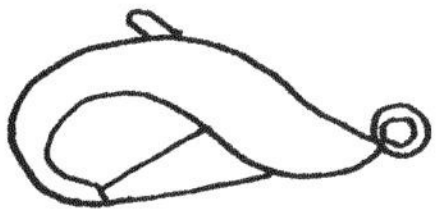

Lobster claw clasp

Barrel clasps, also known as screw-type clasps, consist of two cylinders that screw together. They are available with or without loop ends. Most of the barrel clasps used in the projects in this book have loops. For details on how to attach a screw-type clasp that does not have loops, see the Floating Wood Necklace on page 47.

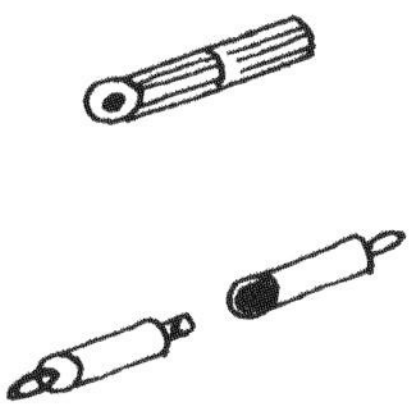

Barrel clasps

Fancy clasps are usually oval or round, with an ornate filigree motif. They come with one, two, or three sets of loop ends to attach one, two, or three separate strands of beads. Use fancy clasps for pieces made of gemstones or pearls, or for Victorian-style jewelry.

Fancy filigree clasp

Miscellaneous clasps include sleek **S-shaped hooks, perforated discs** that you bead yourself, and **toggles.** The toggles consist of a chained piece with a long tube bead or another thin, solid metal piece at one end, which is inserted into a circular piece.

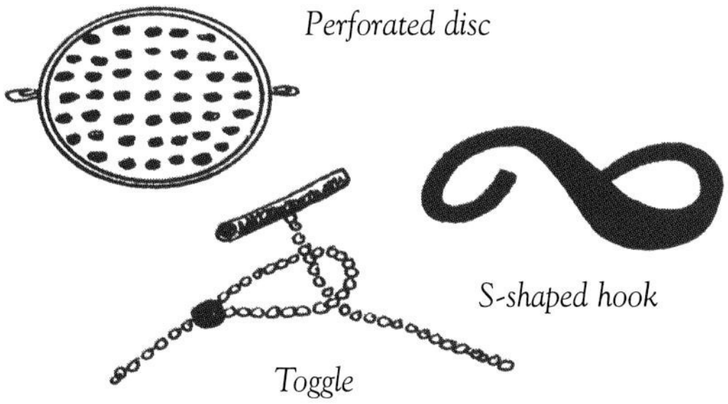

Perforated disc

S-shaped hook

Toggle

EARRINGS

Kidney ear wires, reminiscent of the Art Moderne style of the '50s, are kidney-shaped. They are readily available in silvertone, goldtone, surgical steel, or sterling silver. Dangles are simply attached at the loop.

Kidney ear wires

French ear wires, also called Shepherd's hooks, are currently the most popular hook-style earring finding. Just be careful not to design an earring with too much weight at the front, or the hook will pull out of your ear. French ear wires are available in silvertone, goldtone, and precious metals (sterling silver or 14K gold for sensitive ears).

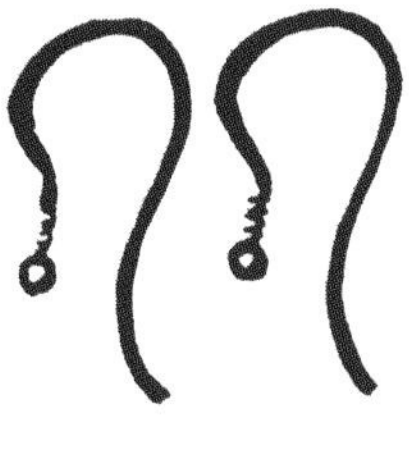

French ear wires

Stud earrings come in two styles: flat-pad post with nut and ball post with nut. Flat-pad posts allow an ornament to be glued directly to the pad. Ball posts come plain or with a small loop at the bottom of the ball to attach a dangle. Both types are available in both precious metals, real and plated.

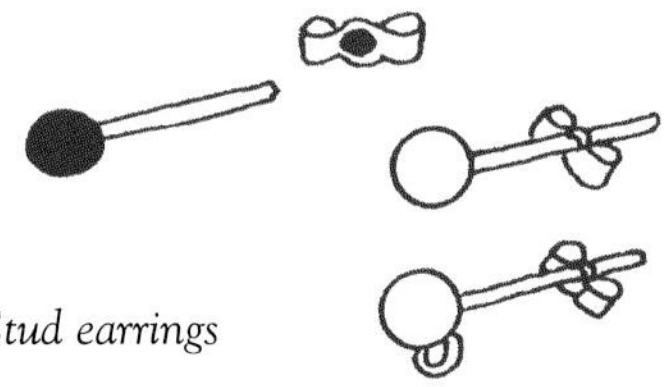

Stud earrings

Clip-on earrings, for those without pierced ears, are available in many styles and metals. Try them on before purchasing them, to be sure they are comfortable.

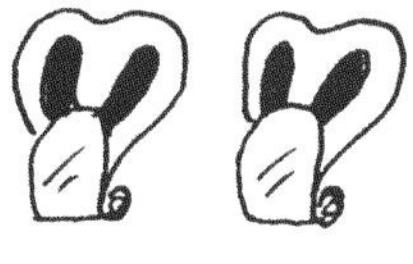

Clip-on earrings

Ear cuffs are semicircular pieces of metal that are worn on the cartilage above the earlobe. The ear cuff is usually worn on one ear only. The hole pierced into the cuff is for attaching adornments.

Ear cuff

MISCELLANEOUS FINDINGS

Crimps are tiny circles of metal (silver or gold) used to attach a clasp to the end of a strand of beads. String the crimp on the end of beaded tiger tail or leather, add the clasp, then reinsert the stringing material through the hole on the crimp. Using jewelry pliers, squeeze the crimp tightly into place. Finally, cut the excess stringing material.

Crimps

Coil ends are spirals of wire used to finish the end of beads strung on leather. For a detailed explanation of how to use these findings, see the Dot Necklace on page 19.

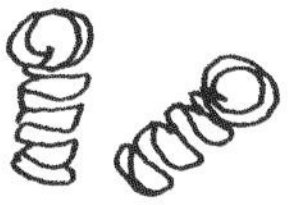

Coil ends

End cones, usually made of silver or goldtone metal, are used to finish the ends of necklaces and bracelets. For details on how to use end cones, see the Fiesta Neckpiece on page 42.

End cones

PIN BACKS

Standard bar-shaped pin backs come in many different lengths. Choose one that is small enough to be concealed behind the pin, yet strong enough to hold the weight of the adornment. Glue or sew it in place slightly above center; if you don't, the top of the pin will tilt forward when you wear it.

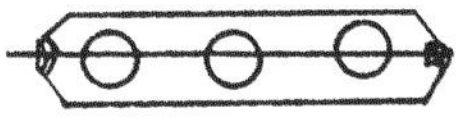

Standard pin back

Circle pin backs have a metal disc permanently attached to the pin. This style is excellent for collage pins and for pins made of heavy components.

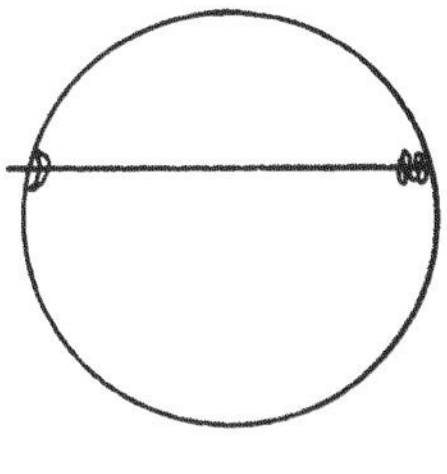

Circle pin back

Stick pins are Victorian in concept but can be used to make a contemporary statement as well. There is a small disc at the top of the long pin on which to build the design. If you like, you can add dangles for interest.

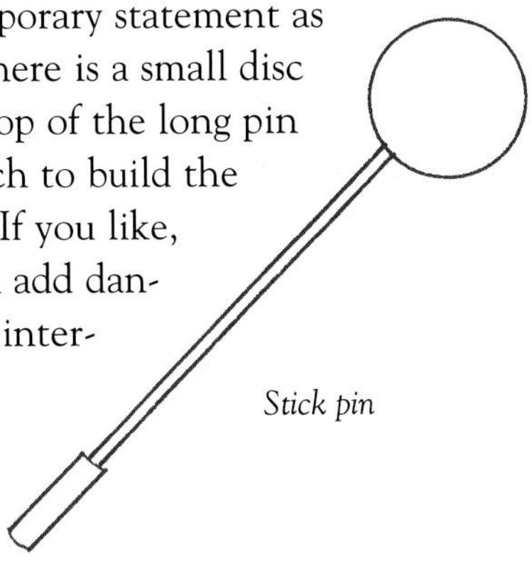

Stick pin

Head to your local sports-supply store for a great selection of tackle boxes—they're perfect for storing beads & findings. While you are there, check out fishing tackle for unusual additions to your jewelry designs.

Other Supplies

THREADS & CORDS

I like to use coated quilting thread, or special beading thread made of 100% nylon, or 100% silk for projects where a fluidity of design is desired. Try to match the color of the thread to the beads, especially if you are using transparent beads.

Tiger tail, a thin steel cable covered with nylon, is very strong. I like it for bracelets, even though it is a bit stiff and does kink. Kevlar, a new synthetic, is available from sporting goods stores. Although it is normally used for stringing bows, many beaders have found this strong material handy for beading. Waxed linen thread has been around for a long time and is still one of the best. Knots hold tightly in place, and it is available in many colors. Try all of the above and any other threads you may come across, and use whatever works best for you.

Leather cord comes in two sizes, 1mm and 2mm. I prefer the thinner kind, since it can accommodate more beads, especially those with a smaller hole. The thicker cord works better with large ethnic beads or with natural objects like seashells. Don't pull too hard when knotting leather cord, or it will break. The ends are either finished with a coil end or simply knotted together.

Cotton cord is available in many sizes and colors. Use it for country-style necklaces or for necklaces with a very simple design.

NEEDLES

Traditional beading needles are extremely thin and long and are well suited for long lines of beading. For most of the projects in this book, I use a #10 quilting needle. This short needle is thin enough to string on the tiniest seed beads.

GLUES & ADHESIVES

Glues should be used very sparingly in jewelrymaking. In the instructions for the projects, when I say glue I mean that you should apply a dot of glue with a toothpick. Professionals use glue sparingly, but I have found that beginners are often unsure of their knots. Once you have gained some confidence, you will no longer need to dot glue on the knots. For this application, I recommend Elmer's, Aleene's, or any other clear-drying white glue. Clear nail polish also works well on knots.

GOOP is an adhesive and sealant specifically formulated for plastic. I have also found it handy for button collage. Use it anytime you are applying heavy objects to a collage piece.

BOND 527, a multipurpose cement, is very strong and easy to apply. Use it in a well-ventilated area; clean up with acetone or fingernail polish remover.

TOOLS

For most beadwork projects, you will need two tools: a pair of round-nosed pliers and a pair of wire cutters. Occasionally, you will find both tools combined into one. (See the pair of lilac-handled jewelry pliers in the color photograph at the beginning of this chapter.)

A utility knife and a pair of quality, full-sized scissors will come in handy for most projects. Cloth scissors are especially useful for fiber work. You may also need a pair of embroidery scissors. I like the fancy stork-shaped kind—they're beautiful, and they work great.

You'll find a padded working board helpful for some beading projects. I use the June Tailor Quilter's Cut 'n Press II, which has a cutting mat on one side and a padded pressing mat on the other. The padded side is printed in one-inch increments, a handy feature when you are beading.

If you're making beads, a wooden or metal meat skewer is indispensable. You can place the beads on the skewer to bake them or let them harden. Skewers are also useful for testing Friendly Plastic or polymer clay for softness, or for moving these malleable materials.

Keep a brayer (small rubber roller, available at art-supply stores) or rolling pin handy for projects that require rolling like polymer clay.

Jewelrymaker's Glossary

Abalone—iridescent pieces of shell, mother-of-pearl; also called paui when blue-green in color

Amber—translucent orange-yellow resin

Amethyst—translucent purple stone

Art Deco—decorative art style expressed by strong linear lines and shapes; popular from 1915 to 1940

Art Moderne—style from the 1950s characterized by kidney shapes, geometrics, and chrome

Art Nouveau—style characterized by soft flowing lines popularized by Alphonse, Mucha, Aubrey Beardsley, and others from 1890 to 1915

Arts & Crafts Movement—reaction to the onslaught of industrial production, a return to handmade

Aurora Borealis—beads with an iridescent finish, literally the Northern Lights

Bangle—endless circle bracelet

Baroque—irregular-shaped bead that is lumpy, not smooth—e.g., freshwater pearls

Beeswax—used to strengthen thread, prevent unwanted tangles, and allow easier threading

Bezel—strip of material, usually metal, used to set cabochon stones

Bicone—bead with a fat center narrowing to each end

Bohemia Glass—beads made in Czechoslovakia by displaced Venetian glass artists

Bolo—leather thong slide, popular with Southwestern attire

Bone—hand-carved beads made from animal bones; some mimic ivory

Bottle glass—African beads made of recycled green and brown glass

Bugle—tube-style bead

Cabochon—gemstone or paste stone with a smooth, rounded top and a flatback. Usually set with a bezel

Calotte—metal crimp used to end a strand of beads

Cane—glassmaking technique in which colored rods are used to create a complex pattern. Also used as a technique for polymer clay

Cap end—metal cap-shaped finding used to finish ends

Ceylon—pearlized coated beads

Chips—small, irregular-shaped semiprecious stones

Citrine—translucent yellow stone; resembles topaz

Clasp—jewelry closure usually made of metal

Crimp—tiny metal ring used to secure ends of jewelry

Crystal—leaded glass beads, usually faceted; also a blanket term for any clear glass bead

Dichroic glass—prismatic glass made of layered oxides

Dog collar—a very close-fitting necklace; 14 inches long

Donut bead—a large, flattened disc with a large hole

Ear cuff—small half-crescent of metal worn on the upper ear

Earring—any ornamental jewelry worn on the ear

Ebony—black wood used for beads; may be carved or smooth

Ethnic beads—primitive beads from Third World countries of many different materials and designs

Eye pin—long wire with a loop at the end

Faceted beads—beads with cut surfaces, like crystals and gemstones

Fetish—primitive charms—for example, the carved turquoise animals used in Native American jewelry

Filigree—ornate, open-weave pattern, often found on metal clasps

Fire polish—glass exposed to extremely high heat to create a special finish

Garnet—translucent terra-cotta red stone

Gold foil—actual gold rolled extremely thin, sold in booklets of "leaves"

Hairpipes—long, ivory-colored bicone beads used in Native American jewelry

Head pin—flat-headed length of wire

Howlite—opaque white stone, often dyed other colors

Iridescent—used to describe any colored bead that looks as if it were dipped in oil to create a special finish

Iris beads—dark beads with a special rainbow coloring

Jade—opaque green stone

Japanese seed beads—size 12 to 16 seeds uniform in shape with a large hole; popular

Jasper—opaque quartz in many colors and patterns

Jump ring—a circle of wire used to attach two jewelry findings

Knot cover—metal clam shell–shaped finisher used to hide knots

Lampwork beads—beads handwrought using a lamp

Lantern bead—cylinder-shaped faceted bead with gold detail

Lapis lazuli—opaque cobalt blue stone often flecked with white

Lined beads—beads whose inside is lined with another color

Linsin—disc-shaped bead with hole running from side to side through center

Luster beads—high-gloss beads

Malachite—opaque emerald green stone, often streaked

Millefiori—glass or polymer clay beads with very ornate patterning resembling bouquets of flowers; literally 1,000 flowers

Moonstone—translucent pearly white stone

Mother-of-pearl—beads or pendants of carved shell; nacre, abalone

Niobium—metal heated to a high temperature to produce iridescent colors (magenta, turquoise, etc.) used for findings

Onyx—translucent black stone, often dyed

Opalescent—reminiscent of the coloring of opals

Opaque—solid-colored beads that don't allow the transmission of light

Peridot—translucent chartreuse green stone

Pony bead—large-holed bead

Rat tail—soft, satiny cord used for jewelry

Rocaille—seed bead with a silver lining

Rondell—flattened, donut-shaped bead

Scarab—beetle-shaped bead of Egyptian origin; signifies long life and rebirth

Sequin waste—perforated leftovers from manufacturing sequins; purchased by the roll or the yard

Spacer—bar with holes used to keep different strands of beads separated; also, term for less important, secondary beads used to build up a design

Split rings—double circle of wire used as a jewelry attachment; alternative to the jump ring

Stabilized beads—powdered gemstones (especially turquoise and opal) mixed with resins to create beads

Striated beads—beads with marblelike streaks of color

Tiger tail—nylon-covered steel

wire used for threading beads

Topaz—translucent golden yellow stone; other colors, too

Tourmaline—translucent stone in many colors; watermelon tourmaline is shaded a striking pink and green

Trade beads—beads actually used for trade; encompasses many types of beads but usually refers to beads from Africa

Translucent—smoky; allows some light to enter but is not clear

Transparent—see-through glass

Tribal beads—beads of specific tribes, or commonly beads of primitive design

Turquoise—opaque blue-green stone; "sleeping beauty" is unstreaked, robin's egg blue in color

Unikate—mottled green and orange semiprecious stone

Victorian—decorative style named after Queen Victoria; heavily ornamented, romantic designs often with motifs of angels, flowers, ribbons

"The ancient and modern art of jewelry making is only one of the many doors to the creative process, but it is a pleasant door, accessible to all, and it has much which commends it as an introduction to the creative way of life. When approached as an experimental art expression it is a thrilling and fascinating activity, admirably suited to the needs of the day because of its unique and versatile qualities. Because of the great freedom which is possible in both design and working processes, and because its functional purposes are not as restricting as are those of other arts, jewelry making probably has no superior as a medium for motivating and developing originality. Its chief function is to give pleasure, and it provides pleasure in the process of creating that pleasure."

D. Kenneth Winebrenner
Jewelry Making

CHAPTER 2
NEW MATERIALS
Sensuous Designs in Plastic & Polymer Clay

New materials open up a whole world of exciting possibilities in design. One such material is Friendly Plastic. Available in flat sticks in various colors, you can make it malleable by heating it in hot water. Then you create the desired form simply by molding the plastic.

Polymer clay is newly popular in the United States, although it has been used in Europe for quite a long time. It comes in a wide variety of colors, which can be mixed to create custom colors as well. Fimo is the popular European brand; it is a bit stiff, but seems to hold fine detail well. Sculpey III, made in this country, is soft and easy to use. Cernit is known for its permanence once baked.

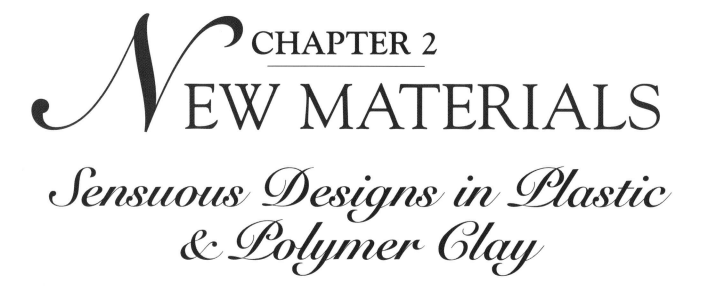

PLASTIC PROJECTS

Nouveau Wave Pins

These molded pins, with their soft, curvy lines, are reminiscent of Art Nouveau jewelry. Just shape the plastic, add faux jewel cabochons and maybe some sequins or other embellishments for fun, and presto! You have works of art!

MATERIALS

Friendly Plastic—metallic colors
Faux jewel cabochons
Sequin waste (optional)
Standard pin backs

TOOLS & SUPPLIES

Aluminum foil
Utility Scissors
Electric skillet or bowl
Wooden meat skewer
GOOP adhesive

PROCEDURE

1. Cover your work surface. Lay out a piece of aluminum foil on which to set the finished pieces.

2. Cut the Friendly Plastic into shapes for the pins. (The pins illustrated here are built up on a half-stick of Friendly Plastic.) You will also need to cut strips and triangles for embellishing the base of each pin.

3. To manipulate the plastic, use water heated in an electric skillet (set on medium), or use very hot tap water in a bowl. You can also place the pieces in an oven (set on low).

4. To make a pin, lay the base piece in the hot water (or in the oven). Use your skewer to check the piece to see if it has softened enough. Watch the piece carefully as it softens; you don't want it to go totally limp. The more you work with Friendly Plastic and learn about how long the softening takes, the more control you will have over the process. Use the skewer on the back side of the Friendly Plastic; any marks you make on the piece will be permanent. (If you are softening more than one piece at a time, do not allow the pieces to touch, or they may become permanently attached.) When the piece is malleable, remove it with the skewer and immediately manipulate it into a wavy structure before it firms up. Anytime you want to manipulate the piece further, simply submerge it in water again.

5. Soften any plastic strips or triangles you wish to use in the design. Place the softened pieces on the base, then submerge the entire piece in the water again so that the pieces bind.

6. To create a bezel to attach the faux jewel cabochon, cut a narrow strip of Friendly Plastic and place it in hot water. Place the embellished base piece in hot water until it softens. (Be careful not to let the base get too soft.) Remove the base from the water, then immediately press the faux jewel in place. Remove the strip from the water and wind it around the base of the jewel. (See Fig. 2.0.) Immediately cut away any excess strip, then let everything harden. If you like, you can soften the Friendly Plastic piece again and add other embellishments, such as sequin waste or more jewels.

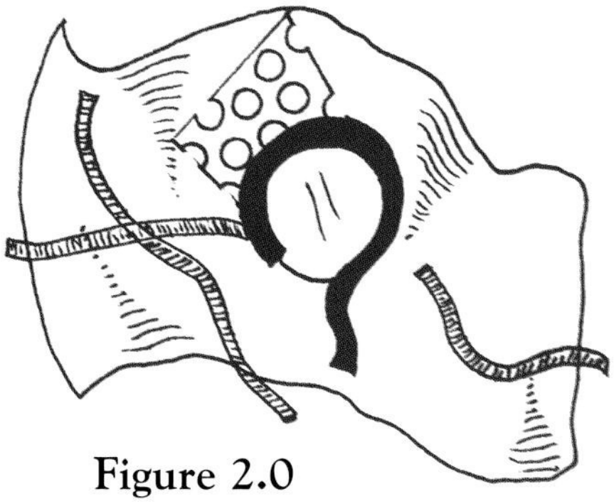

Figure 2.0

7. Glue the pin back to the pin.

> Design jewelry based on a vacation memory. Use brilliant yellow, orange & bright magenta beads to replicate a Hawaiian sunset. A wide range of green seed beads interspersed with sky blue beads could represent a trip to a mystic forest. Use colors to stimulate good memories.

PLASTIC INLAY EARRINGS

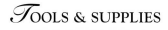

For this modern pair of earrings, you'll learn how to embed the plastic using an inlay technique. You'll also be using cheesecloth to add a nice textural touch. Consider other ways to add texture to your designs—for example, with whisks, wooden blocks, or rice.

MATERIALS

- Friendly Plastic—gold, confetti, purple (or colors of your choice)
- 4 gold jump rings
- 1 pair gold French ear wires

TOOLS & SUPPLIES

- Aluminum foil
- Utility scissors
- Electric skillet or bowl
- Wooden skewer
- Cheesecloth
- Brayer or rolling pin
- Darning needle

PROCEDURE

1. Cover your work surface. Get a small piece of aluminum foil ready so you can place the finished pieces on it to set.

2. Cut two 1½-inch-square pieces of the gold Friendly Plastic. Cut two ¾-inch-square pieces of the confetti Friendly Plastic. Using the triangle pattern shown in Figure 2.1, cut two pieces out of the purple Friendly Plastic.

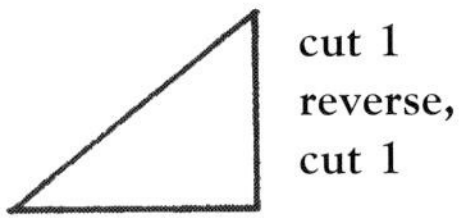

Figure 2.1

3. Read about the basics of working with Friendly Plastic in Nouveau Wave Pins, steps 3, 4, and 5.

4. Lay all of the plastic pieces in hot water. (Be sure they don't touch.) Remove both gold squares when they have softened. Lay a piece of cheesecloth on top of the gold squares, then roll across the cloth with the brayer or rolling pin. Remove the cheesecloth. Lay the gold squares back in the water for just a moment, then remove them. Immediately remove the confetti pieces from the water and set them in place on the gold squares. (Refer to the color photograph for placement.) Then quickly remove the triangles from the water and set them in place. Immediately roll across the pieces to fuse them together before they harden. If, at any time, the Friendly Plastic hardens and does not adhere, place it back in the water to resoften it.

5. Dip the top of each earring into the water. Take the darning needle and create a hole at the center top of each gold square, ⅛ inch down from the edge.

6. Insert a jump ring through the hole on each earring. Attach another jump ring to the first. Add the French ear wire as shown in Figure 2.2, then close the jump ring.

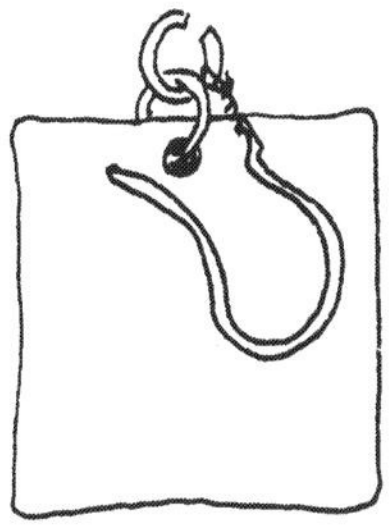

Figure 2.2

Untitled
by Myrna Kanter

This 18-inch polymer clay necklace was made using cane techniques and strung on nylon thread with a sterling silver clasp.

WRAP & ROLL NECKLACE

Make your own plastic beads using a simple wrap-and-roll technique. Although the neckpiece shown here uses a rather large bead, you can make these Friendly Plastic beads any size you like. The finished necklace is 26 inches long with a toggle-style closure.

MATERIALS

- Friendly Plastic—leopard skin (to make 3 beads), dark blue metallic (to make 5 beads)
- Tiger tail
- 2 goldtone crimps
- 38 black beads, 14mm
- 30 gold metal seed beads, size 11
- 5 black tube beads, 1¼" long
- 25 goldtone metal discs, 10mm

TOOLS & SUPPLIES

- Aluminum foil
- Utility scissors
- Electric skillet or bowl
- Wooden skewer
- Jewelry pliers

PROCEDURE

1. Cover your work surface. Set aside a piece of aluminum foil on which to set the finished pieces as they harden.

2. A standard piece of Friendly Plastic measures 1½ inches by 7 inches. For the leopard skin beads, cut the Friendly Plastic as shown in Figure 2.3. Cut the blue metallic piece as shown in Figure 2.4.

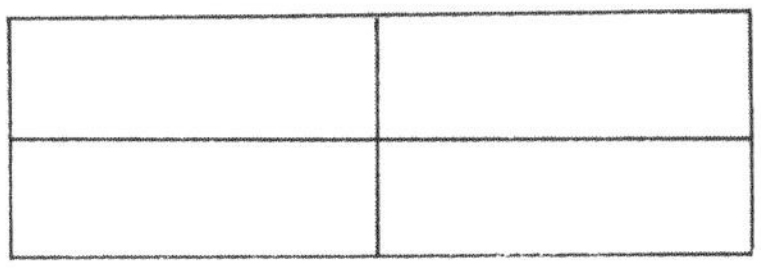

Figure 2.3

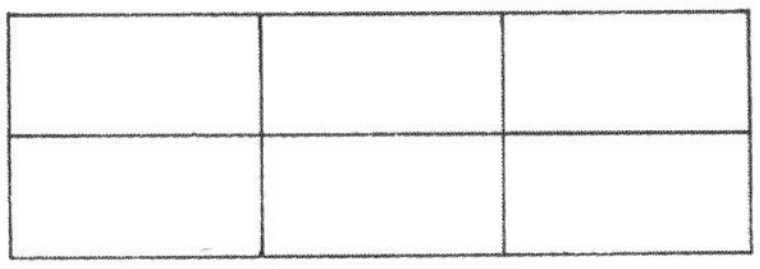

Figure 2.4

3. Read about the basics of working with Friendly Plastic in Nouveau Wave Pins, steps 3, 4, and 5. The secret to making these tailored beads is to leave the Friendly Plastic in the hot water only for as long as it takes to soften the plastic. If you don't leave the plastic in long enough, it won't wrap smoothly and the ends won't stick together. If left in too long, it sticks to the skewer and is difficult to remove. It's a good idea to cut extra pieces of Friendly Plastic and practice on these before proceeding with the project.

4. Soften the plastic pieces in hot water. Remove a piece and wrap it around the skewer, sealing the end. (See Fig. 2.5.) Remove it from the skewer, then place it on the piece of foil to harden. Repeat this step for all of the pieces. For this project, you will need three leopard skin beads and five blue metallic beads.

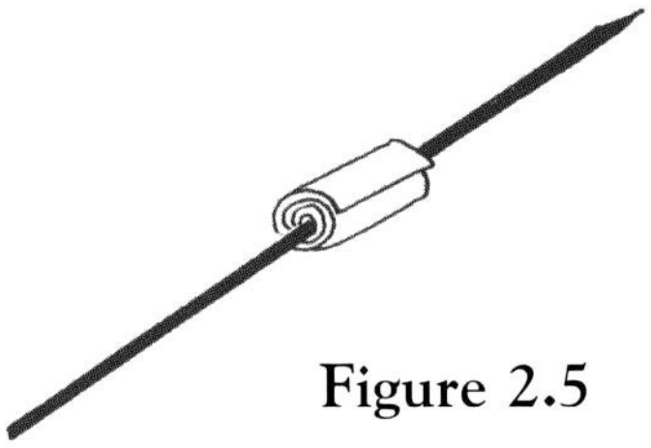

Figure 2.5

5. Cut a piece of tiger tail 36 inches long. String on a crimp, then 1 black bead, 5 gold seed beads, 6 black beads, and 5 gold seed beads. Feed the end of the tiger tail back through the first black bead and through the crimp. (See Fig. 2.6.) Use pliers to flatten the crimp. Trim away the excess tiger tail.

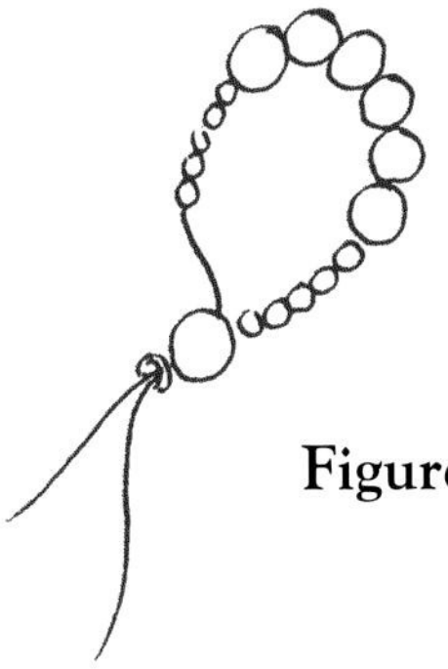

Figure 2.6

6. String on 1 black bead, 1 black tube bead, 5 black beads, 1 black tube bead, * 1 gold metal disc, 1 black bead; repeat from * four times. String * 1 gold metal disc, 1 blue plastic bead, 1 gold metal disc, 1 black bead, 1 gold metal disc, 1 leopard skin plastic bead, 1 gold metal disc, 1 black bead; repeat from last * two more times. String 1 gold disc, 1 blue plastic bead. String * 1 gold disc, 1 black bead; repeat from last * four more times.

7. String 1 gold disc, 1 tube, 5 black beads, 1 tube, 2 black beads, 1 crimp, 1 gold disc, 1 blue plastic bead, 2 black beads, 10 gold seed beads, 1 tube, 10 seed beads. Reinsert the tiger tail back through the beads and through the crimp. Flatten the crimp with pliers. Trim away any excess tiger tail. For extra security, dot the crimps with clear fingernail polish, if desired.

POLYMER CLAY PROJECTS

DOT NECKLACE

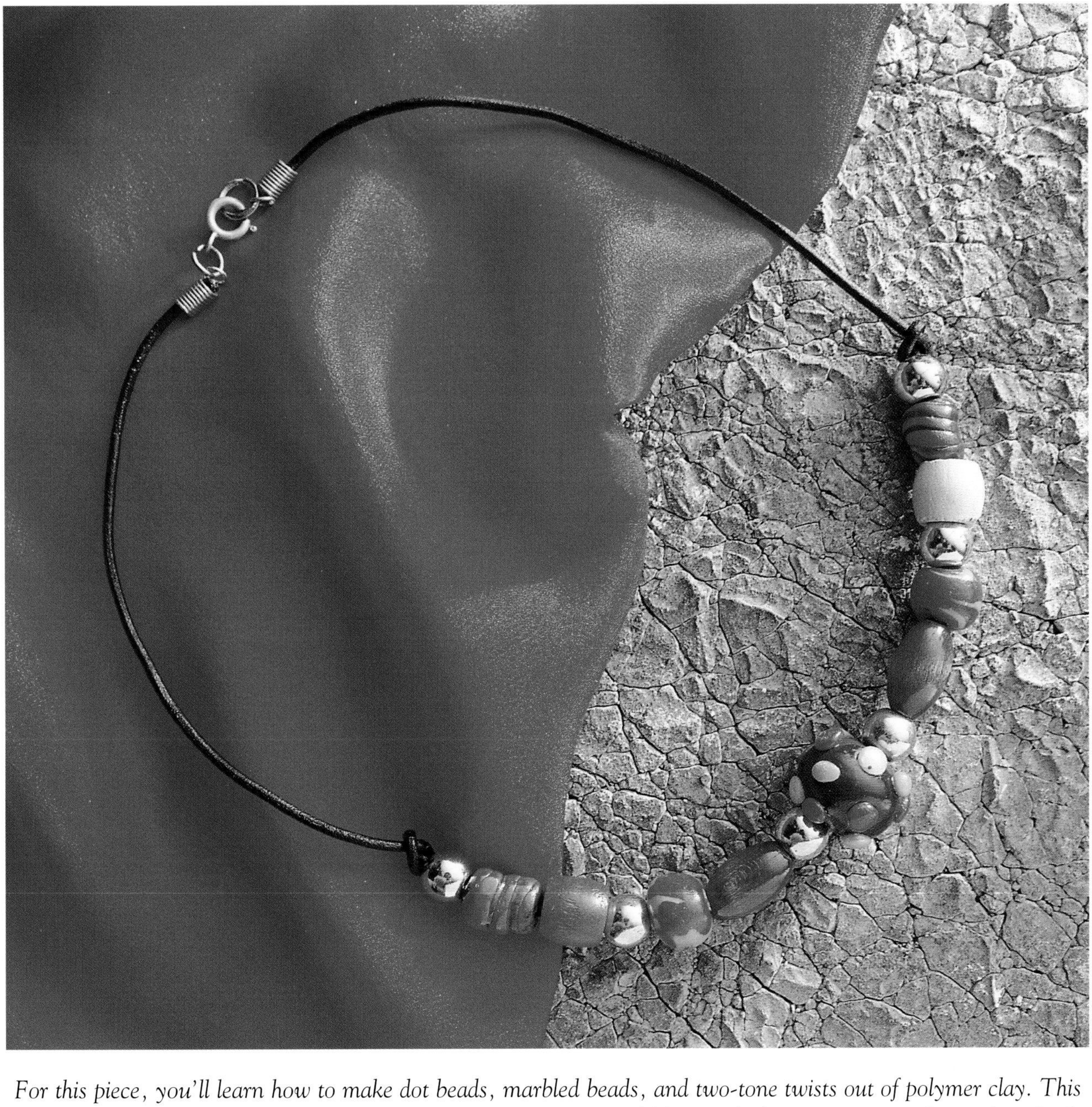

For this piece, you'll learn how to make dot beads, marbled beads, and two-tone twists out of polymer clay. This lovely necklace finishes to a princess length of 18 inches. If you'd like it to be longer, just use a longer length of leather thong and add a few more beads.

MATERIALS

Polymer clay—purple, red, yellow, white (to make 1 dot bead, 2 marbled beads, and 2 two-tone twists)

Leather thong, 20"

6 goldtone beads, 9mm

1 red wooden pony bead, ½" long

1 pink wooden pony bead, ½" long

2 purple wooden oval beads, 1⅛" long

2 goldtone coil ends

2 jump rings

Spring ring clasp

TOOLS & SUPPLIES

Wooden skewer

Aluminum foil

Utility knife

Polymer clay glaze, matte or gloss

Paintbrush (for applying glaze)

Jewelry pliers

PROCEDURE

1. Knead the polymer clay until it softens.

2. To make the dot bead, roll the purple clay into a ball about 2½ inches in diameter. Use the skewer to make a hole. Roll small balls from the red and yellow clay. Make violet by blending ⅔ white and ⅓ purple clay; roll into small balls. Press the small balls of clay onto the large purple ball. Put the dot bead on the skewer and place it on the foil. (See Fig. 2.7.)

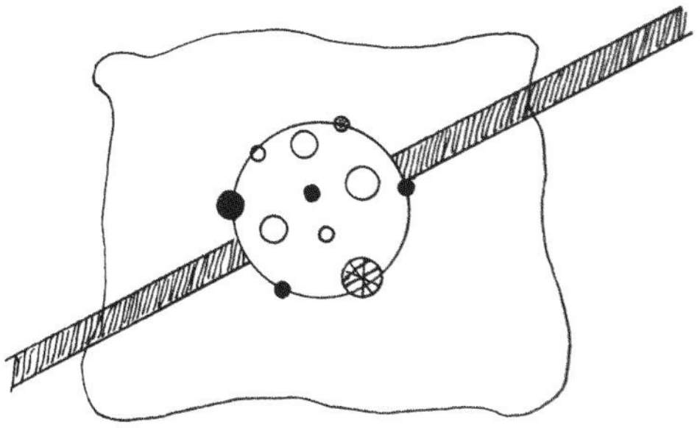

Figure 2.7

3. To make the marbled beads, take equal amounts of red and yellow clay and work the clays together to create a striated effect. Do not overwork the clay, or it will become a solid orange color. Roll the marbled clay into two balls about half the size of the large purple bead. Insert the marbled beads on the skewer. (See Fig. 2.8.) Be sure the beads aren't touching.

4. To make the two-tone twists, lay two equal-sized strips of red and purple clay side by side lengthwise. Pick up the strips and twist them into one strip to create a sensuous form. (See Fig. 2.9.) Cut the twists into two pieces about ½ inch in length, and push them onto the skewer. Make sure none of the beads touch.

Figure 2.9

5. Place the beads in the oven and bake on the lowest setting (275 degrees) for 20 minutes. (When baking polymer clay, remember that thin pieces can burn easily, so watch them carefully and keep the heat low; thicker pieces can withstand slightly higher heat.) Let the pieces cool, then glaze them.

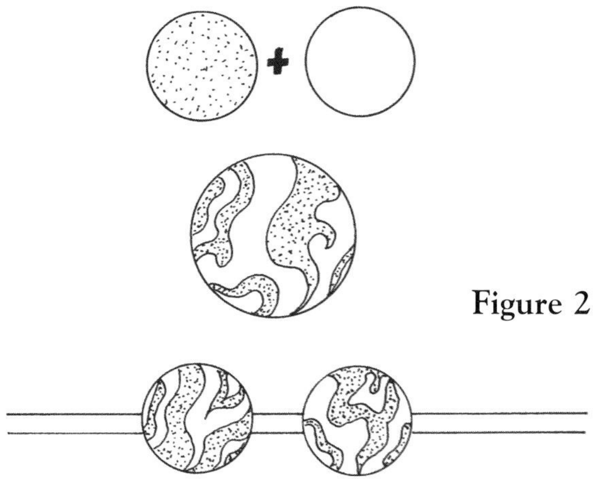

Figure 2.8

6. String the beads on the leather thong in the following order: 1 gold, 1 two-tone twist, 1 red wood, 1 gold, 1 marbled, 1 purple oval, 1 gold, 1 dot, 1 gold, 1 purple oval, 1 marbled, 1 gold, 1 pink wood, 1 two-tone twist, and 1 gold. Center the beads on the thong. Make an overhand knot on either side of the beads to hold them in place and add interest. (See Fig 2.10.)

Figure 2.10

7. Take one of the leather thong ends and fold it over 1/4 inch, then insert it into the coil end. (See Fig. 2.11.) Attach the other coil end. Attach a jump ring to each coil end, then attach the spring ring clasp.

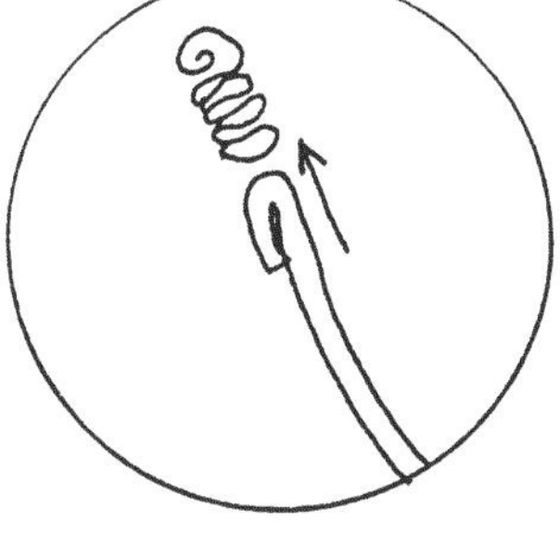

Figure 2.11

IRIDESCENT CHARM BRACELET

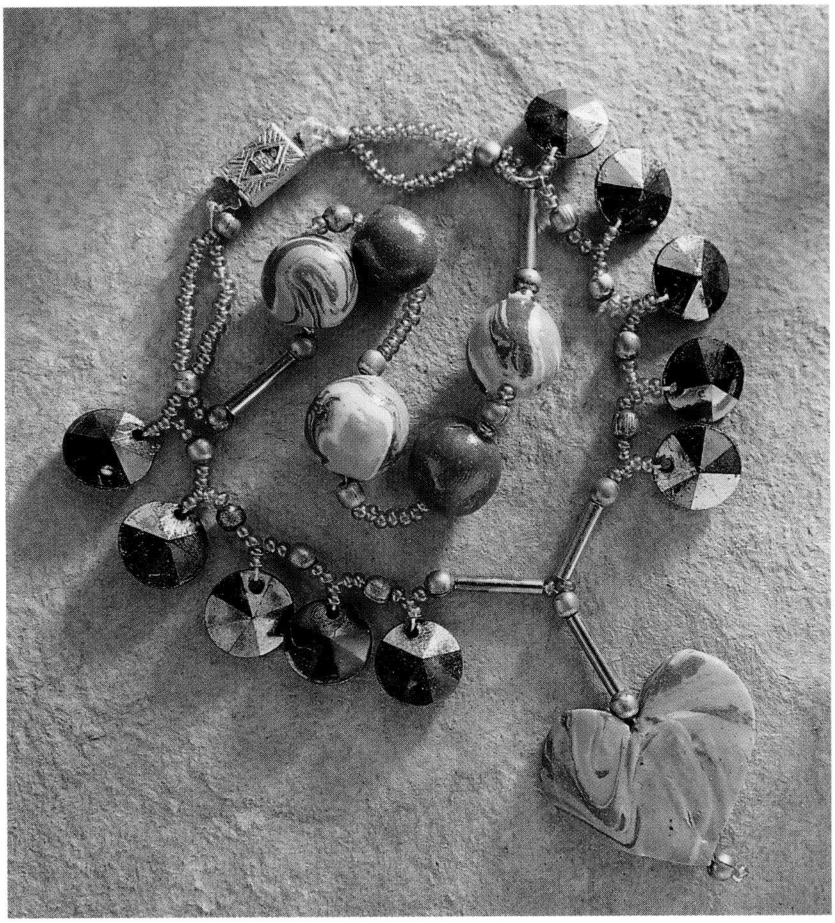

Marbled polymer clay beads and iridescent disc-shaped beads ornamented with a dangling heart charm combine to make this stylish piece. The bracelet fits up to a 7-inch wrist; the charm strand is longer and is designed to drape down onto the back of your hand.

MATERIALS

Polymer clay—pink, white, light blue, burgundy (to make 3 marbled beads, 1 heart, and 2 burgundy beads)

26 goldtone metal beads, size 8

1 tube iridescent seed beads, size 11

10 iridescent faceted discs, ⅜" wide

6 silver tube beads, ½" long

Silvertone fancy box clasp

TOOLS & SUPPLIES

Wooden skewer

Brayer or rolling pin

Tracing paper

Utility scissors

Utility knife

#10 quilting needle

Aluminum foil

Baking pan

Polymer clay glaze, gloss or matte

Paintbrush (for applying glaze)

Quilting thread

June Tailor Quilter's Cut 'n Press II, or padded working board

PROCEDURE

1. Knead the polymer clay to soften it.

2. Take equal-sized pieces of the pink, white, light blue, and burgundy polymer clay. Knead them together to produce a marbling effect, but don't overwork the clay, or you'll end up with a solid color. Roll three large marbled beads, each about the size of a cranberry. Make a hole in each bead with the skewer, then place the beads on the skewer. Don't let the beads touch.

3. Use the brayer or rolling pin to roll out a piece of the marbled polymer clay to about 1⁄16 inch thick. Trace the heart pattern shown in Figure 2.12. Using the knife, cut out the clay heart. Use the needle to create a hole the length of the heart. (See Fig. 2.13.) Lay the heart on a small piece of aluminum foil.

Figure 2.12

4. Roll out two solid-colored burgundy beads, slightly

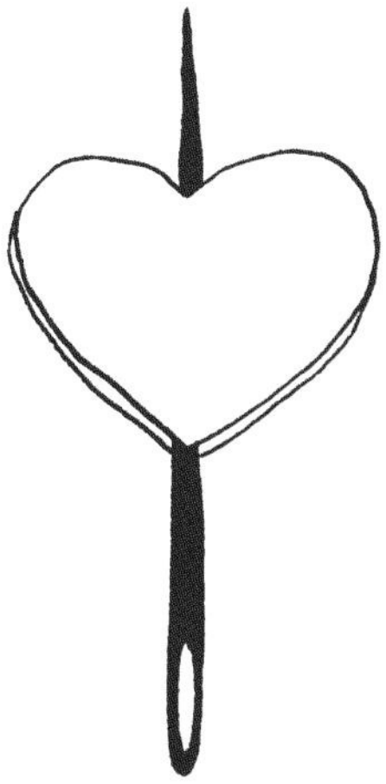

Figure 2.13

smaller than the three marbled beads. Make holes and insert them on the skewer with the other beads.

5. Set the skewer of beads across the baking pan. Lay the heart in the pan and bake in a 275-degree oven for 20 minutes. (For more information on baking polymer clay, see "Dot Necklace," Step 5.) Allow the pieces to cool, then glaze them.

6. Cut a 15-inch length of thread, and thread the needle. For the first bracelet strand (the longer charm strand), string on 1 gold bead and 12 iridescent seed beads. * Add 1 gold bead, 5 seed beads, and 1 iridescent disc, then reinsert the needle back through 3 seed beads and add 2 seed beads; repeat from the * four

more times. Then string on 1 gold bead, 1 tube, 1 seed bead, 1 gold bead, 1 tube, 1 gold bead, 1 polymer heart, 1 gold bead, and 1 seed bead. Reinsert the needle through to the third gold bead. (See Fig. 2.14.) Now repeat the pattern to finish the beading of the other side of this bracelet. Pin the bracelet to a padded working board.

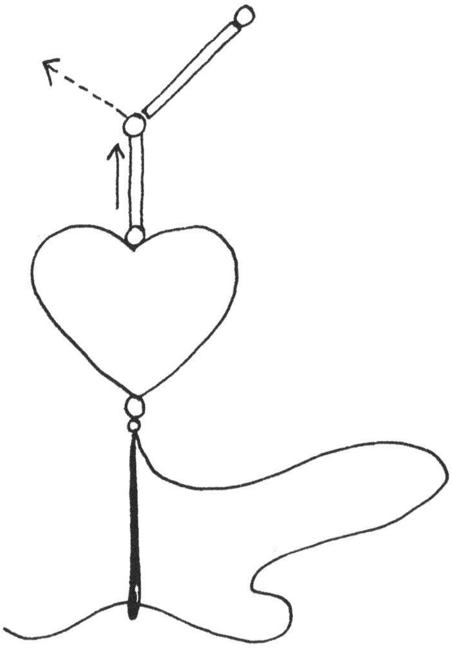

Figure 2.14

7. Cut a 12-inch length of thread, and thread the needle. Insert the needle through the gold bead on the first strand. (See Fig. 2.15a.) String 12 iridescent seed beads, then go through the gold bead on the first strand. (See Fig. 2.15b.) String 2 seed beads, 1 gold bead, 1 tube, 1 gold bead, 1 seed bead, 1 marbled bead, 1 seed bead, 1 gold bead, 1 seed bead, 1 burgundy bead, 7 seed beads, and 1 marbled bead. Repeat the beading pattern.

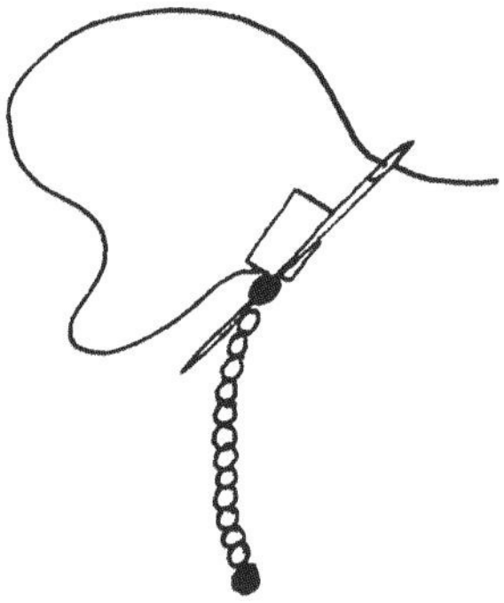

a

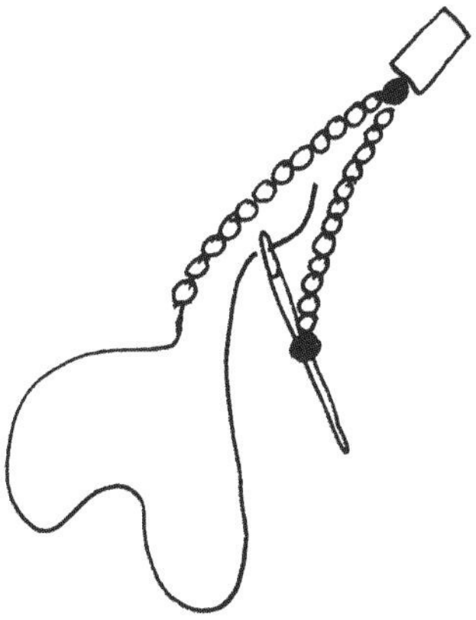

b

Figure 2.15

8. Knot the clasp to the ends. Run the threads back through 5 or 6 beads. Cut away any excess thread.

NOTE: For a nice variation of this piece make a Queen of Hearts bracelet. Just create lots of polymer clay hearts in the colors of the rainbow. String with all golden beads.

Polymer clay emits noxious fumes when baked. Use adequate ventilation—open the kitchen door, or turn on the vent. Always wash your hands to remove any plasticizer residue. Reserve tools & utensils strictly for clay work.

ORNATE BEADED BUTTERFLY PIN

Take a simple motif like the butterfly, and make it special with lots of beading. This project uses just a few beads of many different colors and shapes. If you have beads left over from other projects, use them up by encrusting the butterfly.

MATERIALS

- Polymer clay—pink, turquoise, dark gray, white, maroon, yellow, fluorescent pink, red
- Clear seed beads
- Small tubes (bugles) in blue, yellow, red, and white
- Pin back

TOOLS & SUPPLIES

- Tracing paper
- Aluminum foil
- Brayer or rolling pin
- Utility knife
- GOOP adhesive
- Polymer clay glaze, gloss or matte
- Paintbrush (for applying glaze)

PROCEDURE

1. Knead the polymer clay to soften it.

2. Trace the wing patterns shown in Figure 2.16. Flip the patterns over and trace them again so that you have four patterns to use for the butterfly wings.

3. Lay out the aluminum foil on the work surface. You will be building, then baking, the butterfly on the foil.

4. Roll out the pink clay with the brayer or rolling pin. Using the top wing patterns, cut out the pink clay with the utility knife. Remove the excess clay.

5. Roll out the turquoise clay, then cut out the bottom wings. Add the bottom wings to the top wings to create

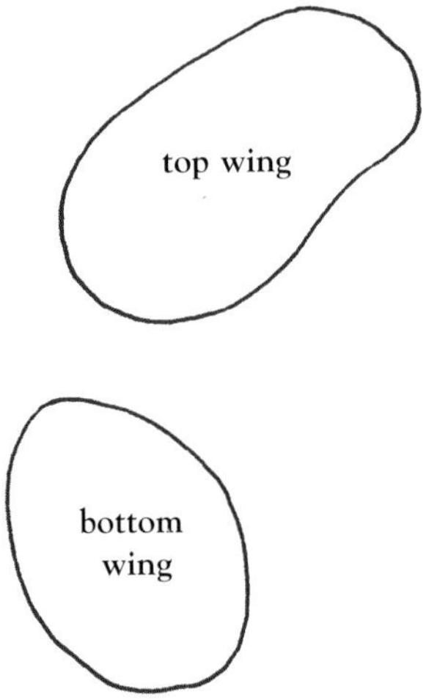

Figure 2.16

a butterfly shape. (See the color photograph for placement.)

6. Blend a piece of gray clay with a small amount of white clay to create a marbled ball. (Don't overwork the clay, or it will turn a solid color.) Pick off two tiny bits of marbled clay. Hand-roll them into strips to resemble butterfly antennae. Set these strips aside for a moment. Shape the remaining piece into a butterfly body about 1¼ inches long. Cut off any excess clay. Position the body onto the butterfly wings. Press the antennae in place at the top of the body.

7. Roll white clay into a tube. Place the clay on the top edge of the top wings as shown in Figure 2.17. Cut off any excess. Place the remaining white clay strip starting at the center of the butterfly, around the edge of the bottom wing, and ending at the bottom of the body.

8. Roll six tiny balls of white clay. Press them onto the wings and flatten. (See Fig. 2.18 or the color photograph for placement.) Make ten maroon balls smaller in size than the white balls. Place one maroon ball on each of the flattened white balls. Place the other four maroon balls on the bottom wings. Roll four yellow balls and place them on the wings. Roll out a long, skinny tube of turquoise clay. Cut four pieces about ⅜ inch in length, and place them at an angle on the top wings. Make eight fluorescent pink balls, and place them on each wing following the pattern. Make two red strips about ⅜ inch long, and place them at an angle on both wings.

9. Firmly press a line of clear seed beads into the white clay lines on the top of the wings and on the edges of the bottom wings. Next, place the blue bugle beads on the turquoise strips on the top wings, and press two yellow bugles into the red strips on the bottom wings. Then add the

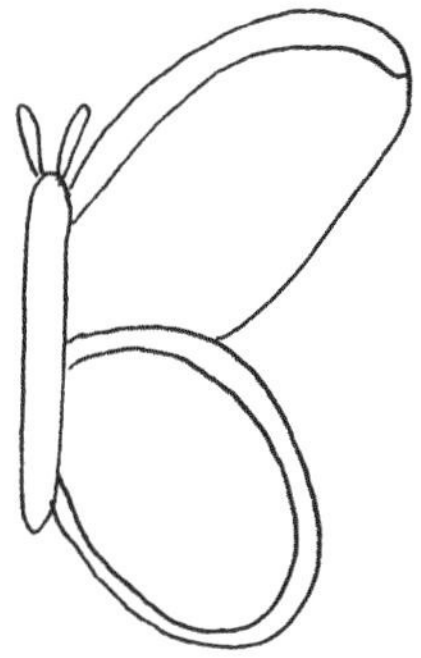

Figure 2.17

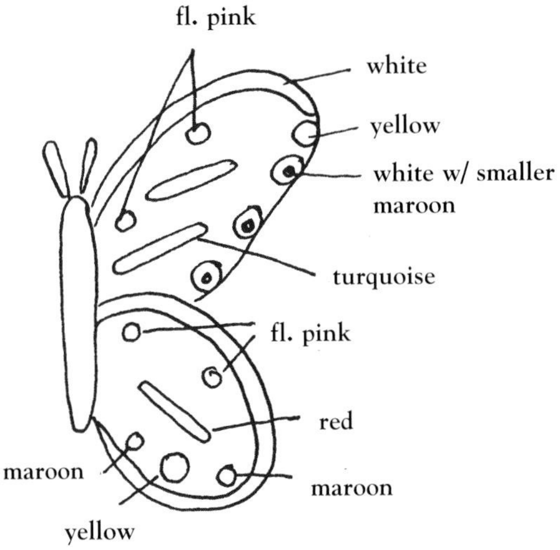

Figure 2.18

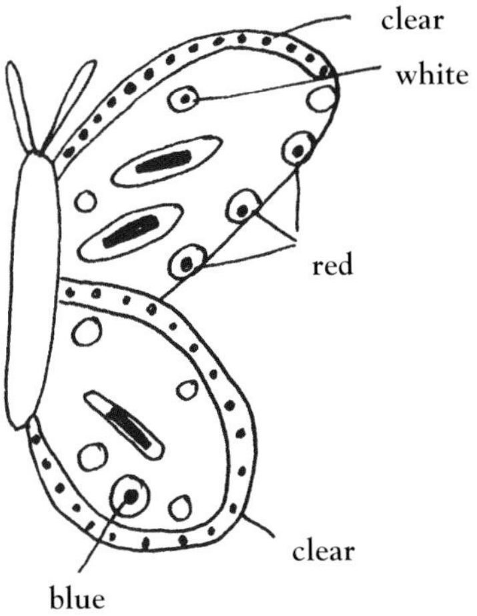

Figure 2.19

remaining beads as shown in Figure 2.19 (or use the color photograph for placement).

10. Bake the piece at 275 degrees for 20 minutes. (See "Dot Necklace," Step 5, for more on baking polymer clay.) If any of the beads have moved, reattach them with GOOP adhesive. Glaze the butterfly, then let it dry. Glue the pin back on the back of the butterfly with the GOOP adhesive.

GOLD-LEAF WAVY DISC NECKPIECE

MATERIALS

Polymer clay—purple, tan, white (to make 5 purple beads, 2 purple end cones, 4 tan wavy discs, and 12 violet beads)

Gold leaf

2 gold metal beads, size 8

1 tube silver metal beads, size 8

10 natural wood beads, size 4mm

Hook clasp

TOOLS & SUPPLIES

Wooden skewer

Beading wire, 2 pieces, each 20" long

Baking pan

Tracing paper

Utility knife

Aluminum foil

Polymer clay glaze, gloss

Paintbrush (for applying glaze)

BOND 527 cement

Quilting thread

#10 sewing needle

PROCEDURE

1. Knead the polymer clay to soften it.

2. Roll the purple clay into five round beads approximately 15mm in size (about the size of a maraschino cherry). Use the skewer to create a hole in each bead, then place the beads on the skewer. Be careful that the beads don't touch.

3. Roll out two conical shapes about 2 inches long and ½ inch wide at the bottom. Insert a wire lengthwise through each cone. (See Fig. 2.20.) Remove a sheet of gold leaf from the booklet, and tear it into small pieces. Roll the end cones and the purple beads in the gold leaf. Add additional gold leaf, if necessary. Place the skewer of beads across the baking pan. Bend the cones into a slightly arched shape, and bend the ends of the wire holding each end cone around the lip edge of the pan. (See Fig. 2.21.)

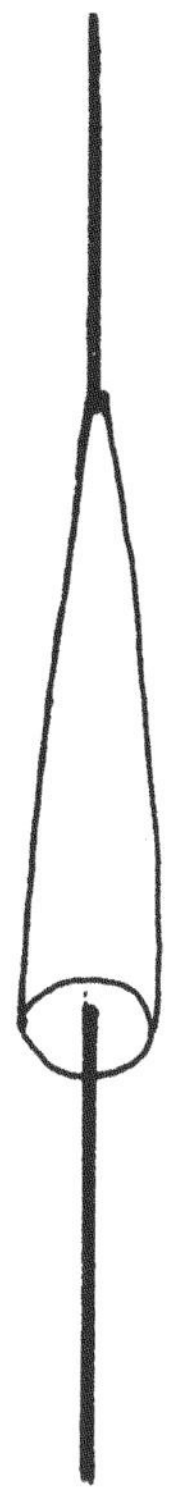

Figure 2.20

Figure 2.21

4. Trace the oval pattern for the wavy discs as shown in Figure 2.22. Cut four discs out of the tan clay, then press them into the torn pieces of gold leaf. Use your fingers to gently pinch the ovals into soft,

Bits of real gold leaf adorn the polymer clay beads, wavy discs, and end cones in this extravagant neckpiece. The wavy discs can be omitted if you prefer a simpler design. The finished length is 25 inches.

sensuous shapes. Use the skewer to make a hole at the top (about ⅛ inch down from the edge) of each disc for stringing. Put the discs on a piece of aluminum foil and set them in the baking pan.

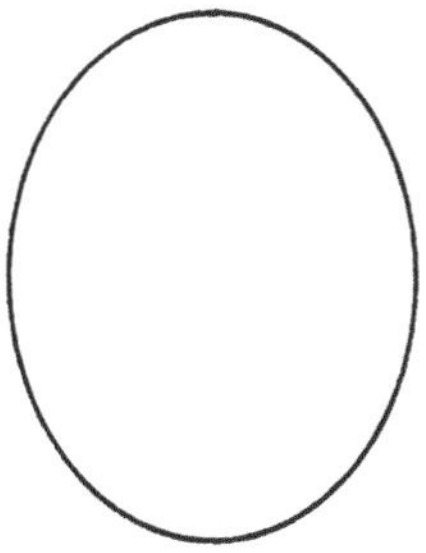

Figure 2.22

5. Create the violet beads by thoroughly mixing together a large piece of the white clay with a bit of the purple. Roll out 12 beads 9mm in size. (See "Bead Sizes in Millimeters" on page 3.) Make a hole in each bead, and place the beads on the skewer so they aren't touching. Lay the skewer across the pan. Bake the clay pieces in the oven at 275 degrees for 20 minutes. (For more on baking polymer clay, see "Dot Necklace," Step 5.) Let them cool, then glaze them.

6. Cut a piece of the thread 32 inches long, and thread the needle. String 1 gold bead, 1 end cone (small end first), 1 violet bead, and 43 silver beads (the equivalent of about 5½ inches). Add 1 violet bead, 1 wood bead, 1 purple bead, 1 wood bead, 1 violet bead, 2 silver beads, and 1 wavy disc, then reinsert the needle through the first silver bead and add one silver bead as shown in Figure 2.23; repeat three more times. Finally, string 1 violet bead, 1 wood bead, 1 purple bead, 1 wood bead, 1 violet bead, 43 silver beads, 1 violet bead, 1 end cone (wide end first), and 1 gold bead.

7. Knot on closure. Feed the thread back through the last gold bead, and cut away any excess thread. Dot the knot with glue.

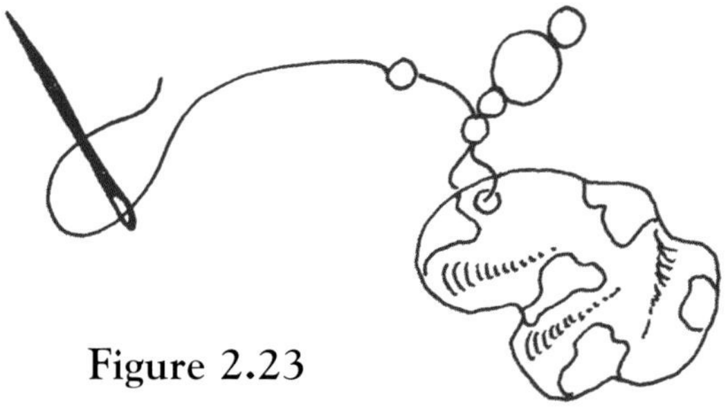

Figure 2.23

Take inspiration from the masters! Both surrealist Salvador Dalí and Kenneth Jay Lané, the noted costume jewelry designer, have made pins featuring a pair of ruby lips. Create your own version in polymer clay.

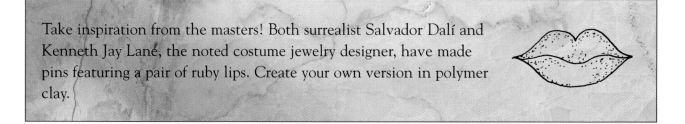

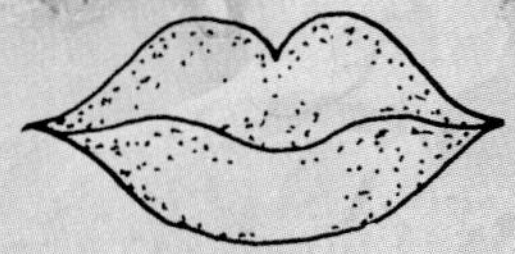

CHAPTER 3

GLORIOUS BAUBLES

The Beauty of Beads & Buttons

You can use seed beads to create a sophisticated brooch or even an exotic Aztec flame-design necklace. Don't have time to bead? Dig through your stash of interesting buttons, and give one of the button projects a try. You'll be amazed at how easy it is to create stunning jewelry with just a few buttons and a little imagination.

BEAD PROJECTS

EBONY TRIANGLE PIN

This striking, sophisticated pin is made of seed beads and long aurora borealis tubes. The beads are sewn to a cloth base using a short stab stitch. Consider using other motifs—squares, rectangles, octagons, hearts, or even fantasy shapes.

MATERIALS

- Black wool felt, 3" × 6"
- 6 aurora borealis tube beads, 1½" long
- 1 tube iridescent violet seed beads, size 11
- 1 tube black seed beads, size 11
- Standard pin back, 1" long

TOOLS & SUPPLIES

- Tracing paper
- Utility scissors
- Cloth scissors
- #10 quilting needle
- Black quilting thread, or uncoated thread drawn through beeswax

Beads on the cheap! Look for old beads at garage sales & flea markets. You won't find single beads. Instead, look for necklaces & bracelets made of glass beads (glass is cold to the touch; plastic is warm). Don't take apart any pieces that have collectible value—preserve them as is & add them to your collection.

PROCEDURE

1. Trace the triangle pattern shown in Figure 3.0, and cut it out with utility scissors. Cut two triangles from the wool felt using the cloth scissors. Set one triangle aside for the pin backing.

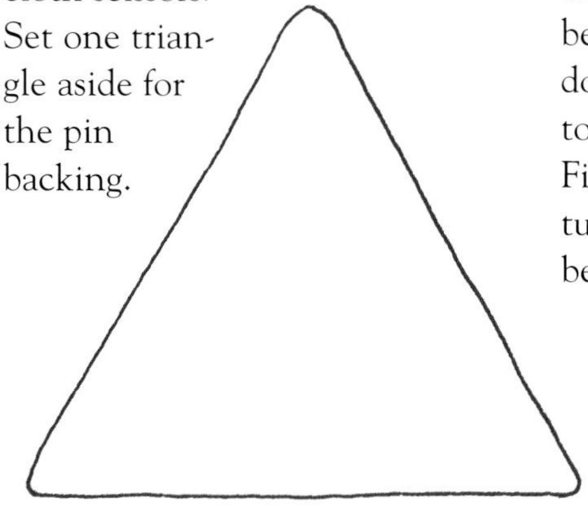

Figure 3.0

2. Thread the needle with 20 inches of the thread, then knot the thread end. Bring the needle through the back of the wool triangle and sew the tube beads in place—first the inside three, then the outside three.

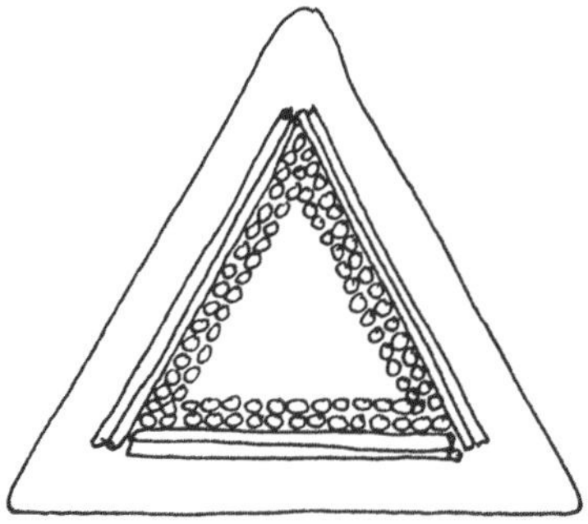

Figure 3.1

3. Working on the inside triangle created by the tubes, sew on two rows of iridescent seed beads, as shown in Figure 3.1, using the stab stitch. (See Fig. 3.2.) To do the stab stitch, bring the needle up through the cloth, slip on a bead, then return the needle down through the cloth as close to the first thread as possible. Fill in the corners between the tube beads with iridescent seed beads. (See Fig. 3.3.)

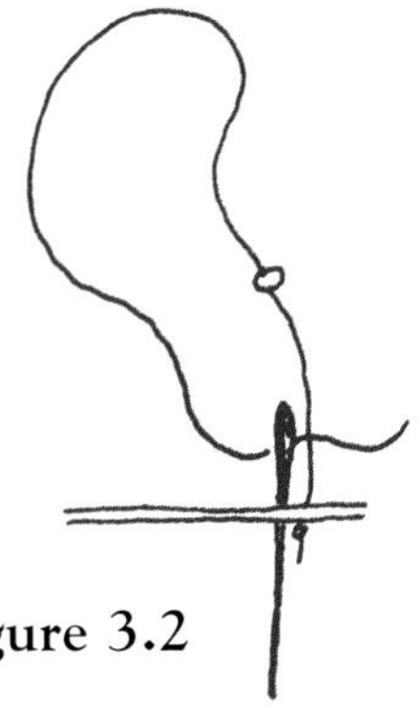

Figure 3.2

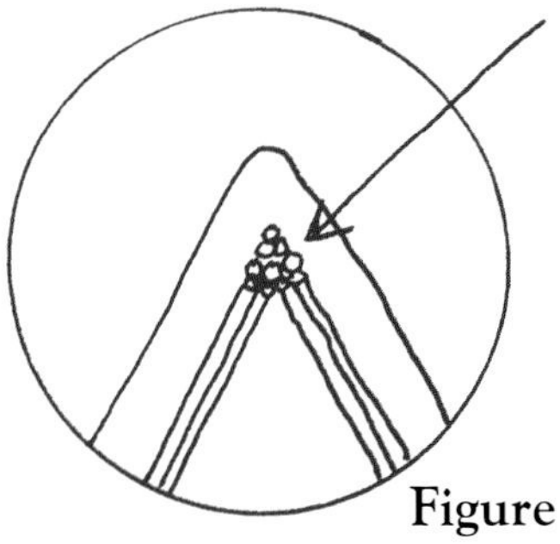

Figure 3.3

4. Turn the beaded triangle over and clip away any excess thread. Place the other wool felt triangle on the back of the beaded triangle. Insert the threaded needle between the front and back wool triangles, coming up very close to the edge of one of the tube beads. (See Fig. 3.4a.) Slip on 5 black seed beads, bring the needle around the edge of the triangle, and bring the needle up very close to the first strand of 5 seed beads to give the piece a clean, finished edge. (See Fig. 3.4b.) Continue the beaded edging around the entire triangle. Hide the knots between the felt layers whenever possible.

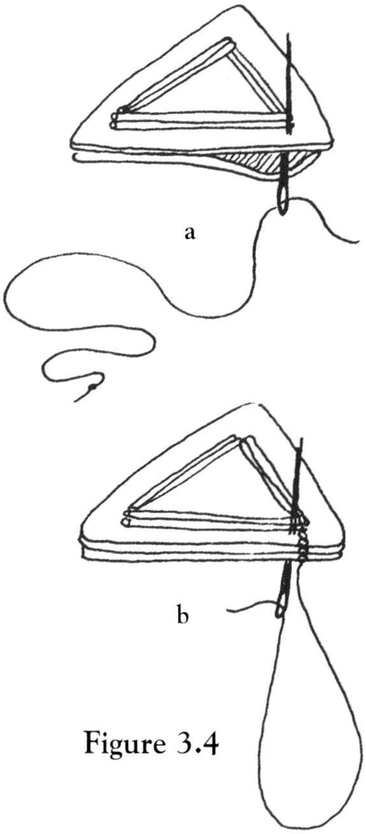

Figure 3.4

5. Sew the pin back on the back of the pin.

AZTEC BEADED COLLAR

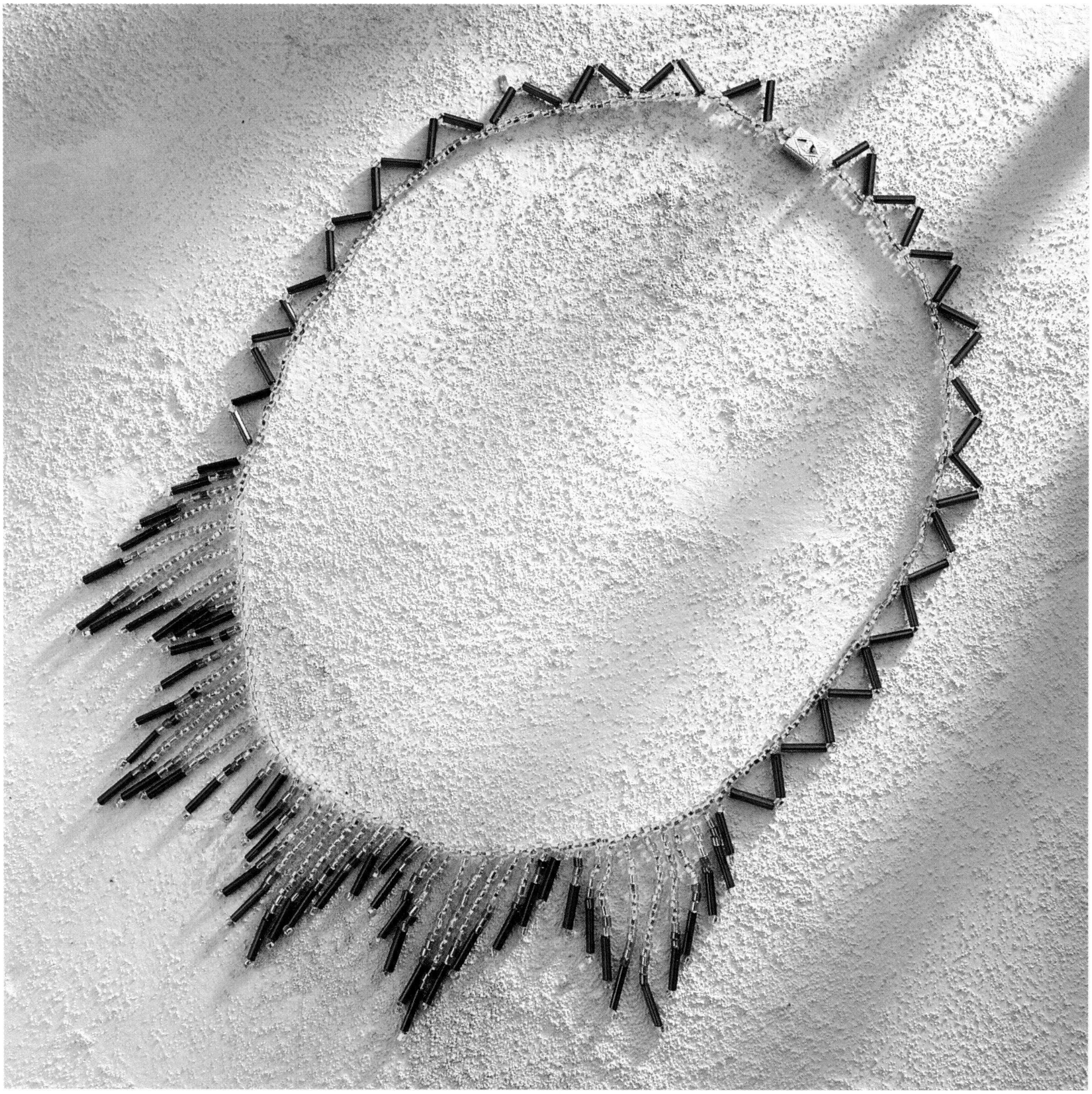

This beautiful piece, which measures approximately 24 inches long, uses a beaded flame-fringe technique and triangles made of bugle beads. Although this design looks complicated and time-consuming, it works up faster than you would imagine. To help make the work go even faster, I've provided both the total number of beads and their equivalent in inch measurements for long beaded lengths. That way, if you forget how many beads you've strung, you can use a ruler instead of recounting the beads.

MATERIALS

1 tube navy blue bugle beads, 5/16" long

2 tubes golden yellow seed beads, size 11

1 tube multicolored seed beads, size 11

Silvertone box clasp

TOOLS & SUPPLIES

1 spool quilting thread

Long straight pins

June Tailor Quilter's Cut 'n Press II, or padded working board

#10 quilting needle

BOND 527 cement

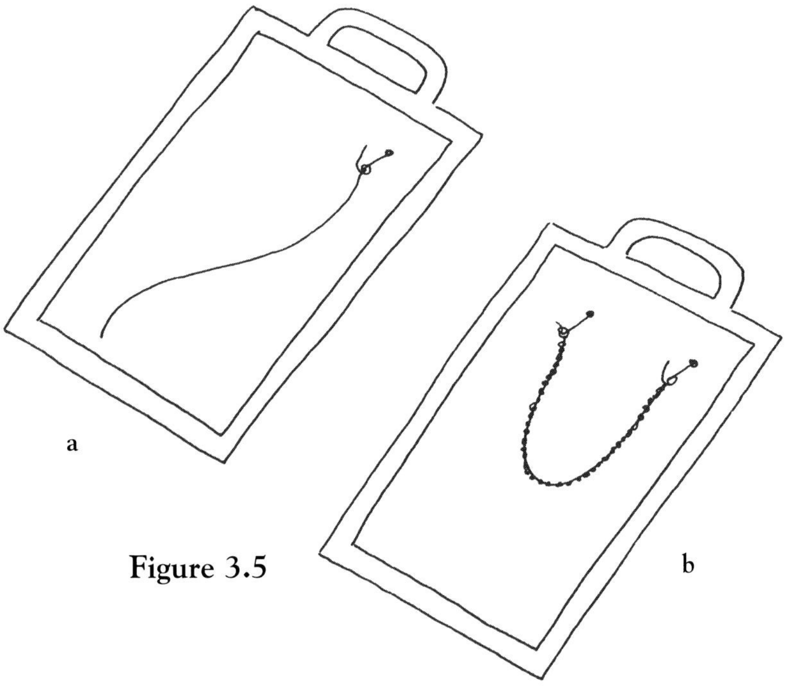

Figure 3.5

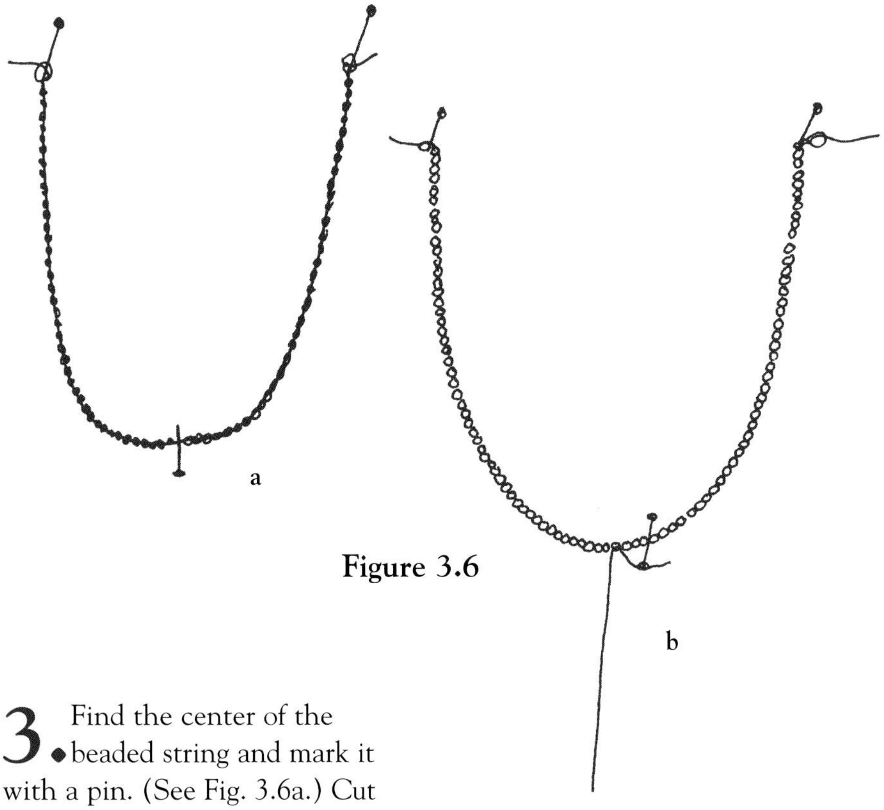

Figure 3.6

PROCEDURE

1. Cut a 30-inch length of thread. Wind one end of the thread around a long straight pin, and insert it into the padded working board. (See Fig. 3.5a.) Put the needle on the other end of the thread.

2. Presort the seed beads, discarding any that are misshapen or that have indistinct holes. String on 274 (20 inches) of golden yellow seed beads. Remove the needle. Wind the thread end around a pin, and insert it in the padded working board. (See Fig. 3.5b.) You now have the basic structure on which to work the Aztec design.

3. Find the center of the beaded string and mark it with a pin. (See Fig. 3.6a.) Cut a 12-inch length of thread and insert it through the center bead so that the ends are even. Wind the right-hand piece of thread around a pin and insert it in the padded working board. (See Fig. 3.6b.)

4. Add the needle to the thread. For the first row, string 12 golden yellow beads, 3 multicolored beads, 1 blue bugle bead, and 1 golden yellow bead. Reinsert the needle through the bugle and the rest of the beads. (See Fig. 3.7a.) Pull the thread taut, then insert the needle through the second golden yellow bead on the structure strand. (See Fig. 3.7b.) Again, pull the thread taut, adjusting the strung beads as necessary.

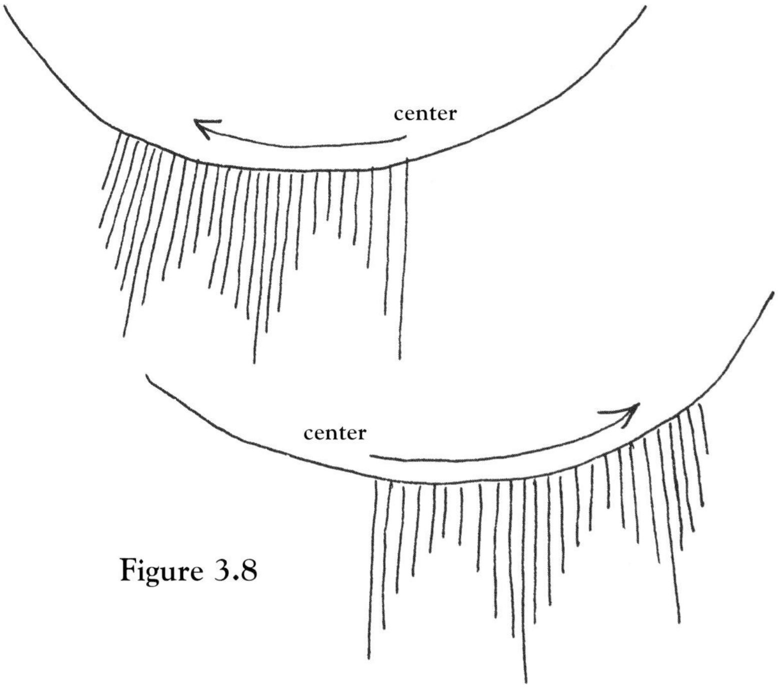

Figure 3.8

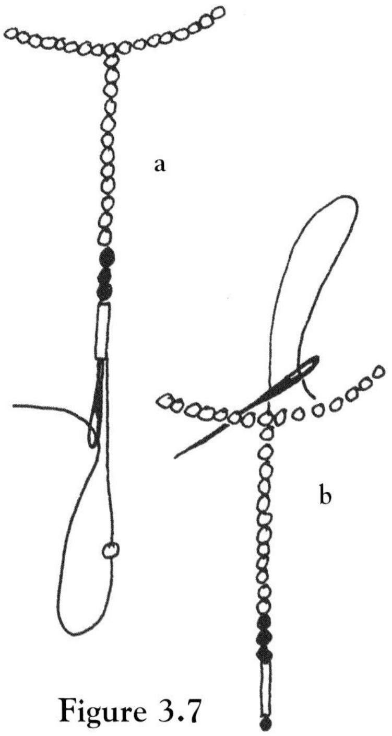

Figure 3.7

5. Continue with the design by working all of the left-hand flame fringes, then unwinding the thread from the pin and working all of the right-hand flame fringes. (See Fig. 3.8.)

Ice Storm
by Bette M. Kelley

This embellished choker necklace is done in glass beads using the techniques of netting, ladders, and kinky fringe.

Use the following illustration and chart for the flame fringes:

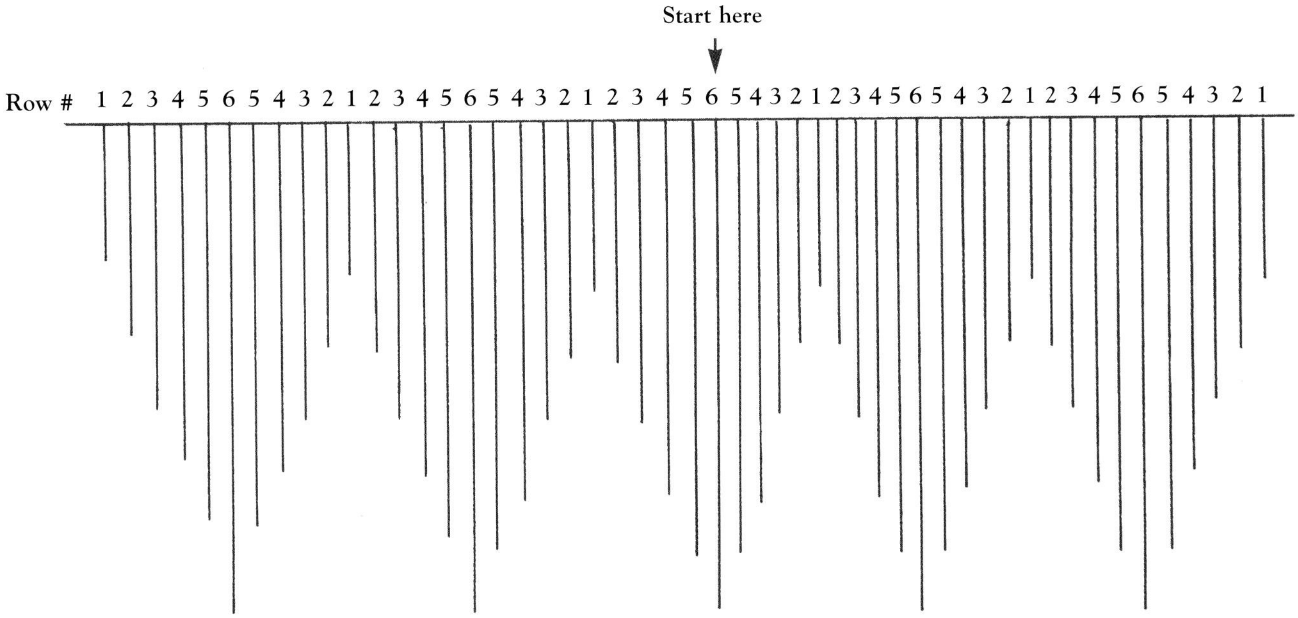

Figure 3.9

BEADING TABLE

	Row 1	Row 2	Row 3	Row 4	Row 5	Row 6
Golden yellow	12	8	4	3	1	1
Multicolor	3	3	3	3	3	0
Blue tubes	1	1	1	1	1	1
Golden yellow	1	1	1	1	1	1

Work the fringes using 12-inch lengths of thread. Whenever you run short of thread, tie on a new 12-inch piece using a square knot, as shown in Figure 3.10, then trim away the excess. When you have finished the flame fringes, do not cut the thread—you will need it for the zigzag border.

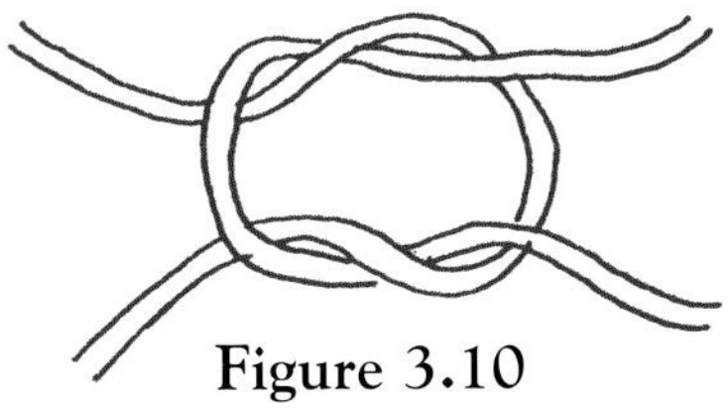

Figure 3.10

6. Using thread left over from the flame pattern, insert the needle two beads over on the structure strand, then string on 1 bugle, 1 golden yellow bead, and 1 bugle. (See Fig. 3.11.) Reinsert the needle eight golden yellow beads away. Bring the needle out and continue the pattern to the end. Work the same zigzag border on the other side of the necklace. Remove the needle.

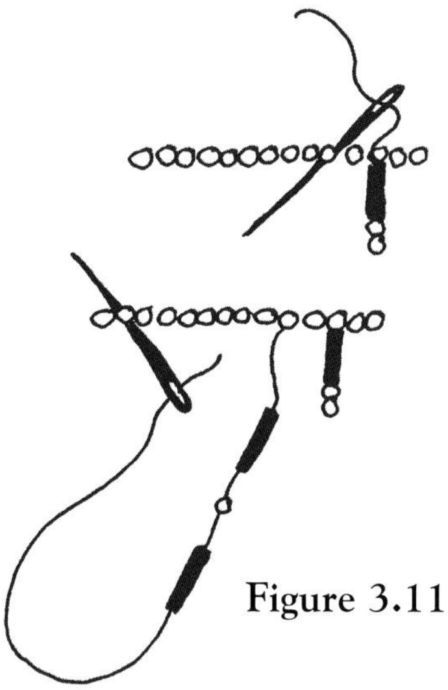

Figure 3.11

7. Double-knot the thread ends of the structure strand and the zigzag border together on each side of the necklace. (See Fig. 3.12.) Then knot each end of the necklace to the clasp. Cut off the thread ends, leaving a 2-inch tail. On both sides of the necklace, place each thread on the needle and reinsert the needle through the strung beads. Dot the knots with glue.

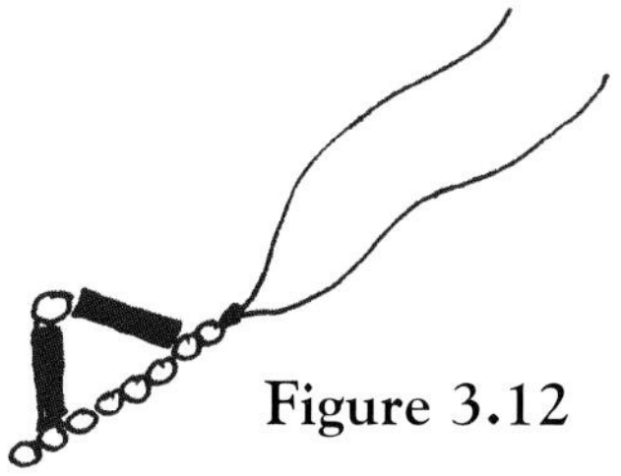

Figure 3.12

MEMORY WRAP BRACELET

MATERIALS

Beads (coordinate by color, shape, type, or simply use whatever you have)
Memory wire (a special wire that comes precut to size and has "memory," always returning to its original shape)
Charms (optional)

TOOLS & SUPPLIES

Jewelry pliers
Jump rings (optional)

PROCEDURE

1. Select one bead as the focal point. Place it on the wire, then put the wire on your wrist and move the focal point bead to the top of your wrist. Hold the bead in place and remove the wire from your wrist. Now add beads on either side of the focal point bead. Anytime you want to check the placement of the beads, put the wire back on your wrist.

2. Once you have added all the beads, take the jewelry pliers and turn the end of the wire back into a loop to act as a stopper. Be sure the loop faces away from the wrist. Otherwise, it will dig into your wrist when you wear the bracelet. (See Fig. 3.13.)

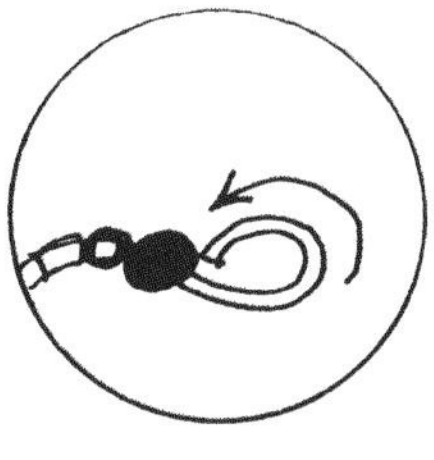

Figure 3.13

3. If you like, you can use jump rings for attaching charms from each of the end loops.

Show off your collection of unique beads in this wrap-around bracelet. Here's your chance to unearth all of those beads left over from other projects and to display some of the more unusual beads you've collected over the years. Long beads (over ¾ inch) tend to distort the wire, so save them for another design. Otherwise, you can use almost any size bead—just be sure the bracelet wraps comfortably around your wrist.

This is one of the easiest projects in the book. Once you've tried it, you may catch the fire and end up creating gobs of memory wraps!

Visit every bead shop in your locality & on your travels. Each bead shop has its own flavor. You'll find the beads are as individual as each shop owner.

BUTTON PROJECTS

ANTIQUE BUTTON BRACELET

In this project, distinctive buttons from an earlier time—when buttons adorned every garment—are refashioned into a charming bracelet. If you don't have a stash of old buttons, look for them at estate or garage sales. For maximum interest, try using one button of each style. You may also want to consider using both goldtone and silvertone jump rings on the same bracelet to pick up the colors in the buttons. Glue large jump rings to the buttons, then use tiny (4mm) jump rings to connect the buttons together.

PROCEDURE

1. Arrange the buttons in any order you like. Mix colors, shapes, and styles for an intriguing design.

2. Turn the buttons over. Place the jump rings so that the same amount of each ring shows on either side of the button when it is turned right side up. (See Fig. 3.14.) Glue

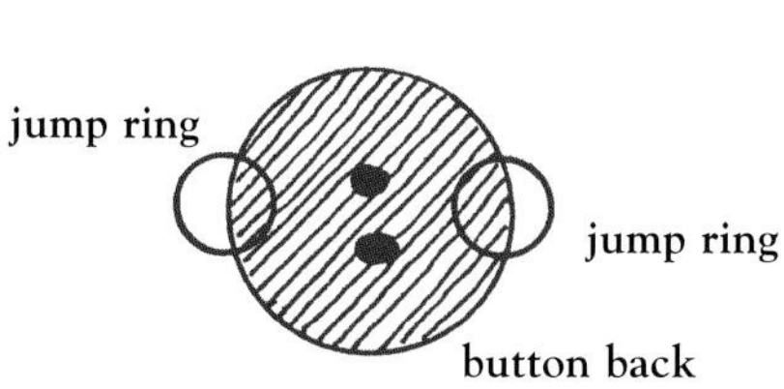

Figure 3.14

MATERIALS

Collection of same-size buttons (e.g., eight ½" buttons for a 7" bracelet, or seven ¾" buttons for an 8" bracelet)

Silvertone or goldtone jump rings, 14mm

Clasp, silvertone or goldtone, spring ring or lobster claw

TOOLS & SUPPLIES

BOND 527 cement

Jewelry pliers

the jump rings in place, then let them dry thoroughly.

3. Using jewelry pliers, open a jump ring and slip it onto the adjoining buttons. (See Fig. 3.15.) Connect all of the buttons together with jump rings. Attach the clasp onto the bracelet.

Figure 3.15

COLLAGED BUTTON PINS WITH OPTIONAL LASSO

Group a cluster of nifty buttons on a special pin back. It's that easy to create splendid jewelry! And while you're at it, why not string buttons on a long golden cord to wear with the collaged pin? You can create many different looks with this combination of lasso and pin. (See Fig. 3.16.)

Figure 3.16

MATERIALS

Buttons—all one color; different sizes and shapes

Circle pin back, 24mm

MATERIALS FOR OPTIONAL LASSO

Small buttons

1 spool heavy gold thread or cord

TOOLS & SUPPLIES

GOOP adhesive

Scissors or utility knife

Cardboard (for optional heart-shaped pin)

Cloth scissors (for optional lasso)

PROCEDURE

1. Arrange the buttons any way you like on the pin back, then glue them in place. Or, if you prefer a heart-shaped pin, cut out a cardboard heart using the pattern shown in Figure 3.17. Glue the cardboard to the circle pin back and let it dry. Arrange the buttons using the largest ones on the bottom and working to the smallest that will accent the design. When you have a design you are pleased with, glue the buttons in place.

Figure 3.17

2. If you'd like to make the lasso, take a 50-inch length of the heavy gold thread and tie on the small buttons using an overhand knot. (See Fig. 3.18.) Use as many or as few buttons as you like. (The lasso shown in the color photograph has thirty ⅜-inch buttons spaced randomly at 1½- to 1¾-inch intervals.) To finish, tie the cord into a square knot and trim away the excess thread. The finished lasso is about 48 inches long.

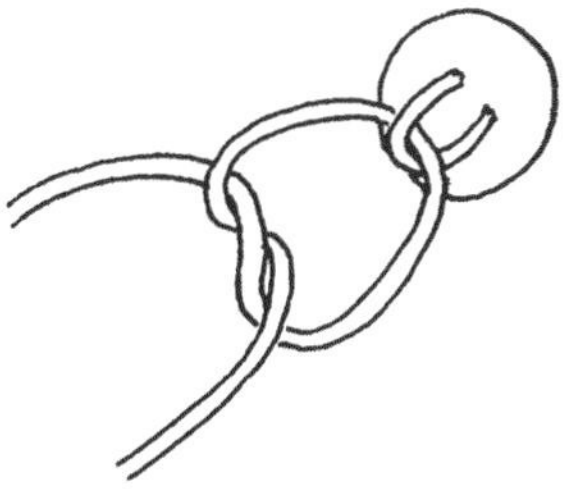

Figure 3.18

CHAPTER 4

TRADITIONAL MATERIALS

Expressions in Fiber, Wood & Paper

Although fiber, wood, and paper are all traditional materials, you can push them to the limit and create new ways to express their beauty. In the hands of a modern jewelrymaker, a piece of cotton cloth or lush velvet—embellished with vibrant colors and beads or other objects—can take on an exciting contemporary look. Fiber can also refer to the actual yarn from which whole cloth is made. Check out the flirty neckpiece made of the new Fiesta thread. Wood is nothing new, but used imaginatively, it can transform a plain necklace into a modern-day piece of art. Even paper, an everyday material, can be used to create distinctive jewelry.

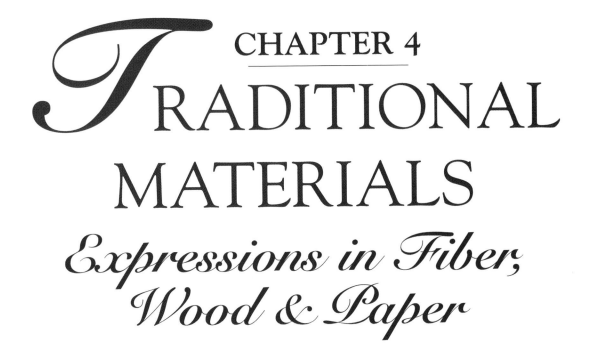

FIBER PROJECTS

FIESTA NECKPIECE

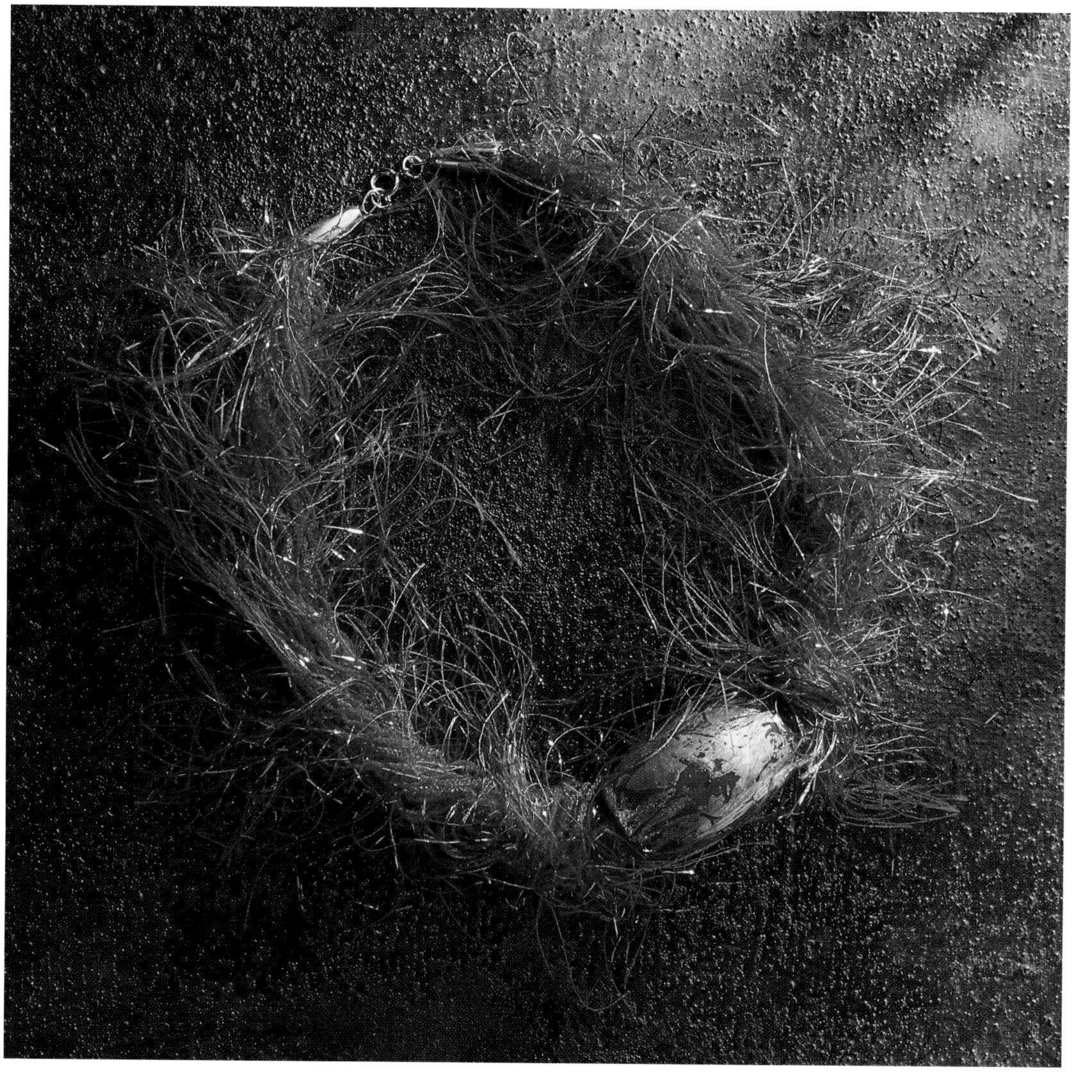

This piece uses an attractive textural thread called Fiesta, manufactured by Madeira. It comes in many intense colors, as well as a multicolored nonmetallic version. The neckpiece is beautiful enough to be worn alone, but you can add a wooden bead done in Renaissance Gold for a little eye-popping punch.

MATERIALS

1 card Fiesta thread, #9 purple
2 goldtone head pins, 3" long
2 goldtone end cones
2 jump rings
Spring ring clasp
1 large wooden bead (optional)

TOOLS & SUPPLIES

Piece of cardboard, 4" × 20", or June Tailor Quilter's Cut 'n Press II
Cloth scissors
Wire cutters
Jewelry pliers
White glue
Scotch tape

OPTIONAL BEAD SUPPLIES

1 jar Renaissance Foil Sealer (available at craft stores)
1 jar Renaissance Foil Italian Red Base Coat
1 jar Renaissance Foil Adhesive
1 sheet Renaissance Foil
1 jar Renaissance Foil Baroque Brown Antique
Paintbrush, #6 flat
Piece of wire, 5" long

PROCEDURE

1. Tape one end of the Fiesta thread to the cardboard piece (or to the June Tailor Quilter's Cut 'n Press II). Wrap the thread firmly, but not too taut, around the cardboard 13 times. Cut the thread from the skein. (See Fig. 4.0.)

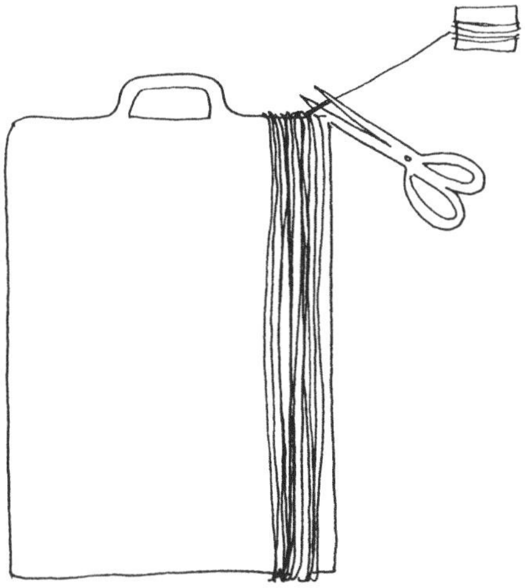

Figure 4.0

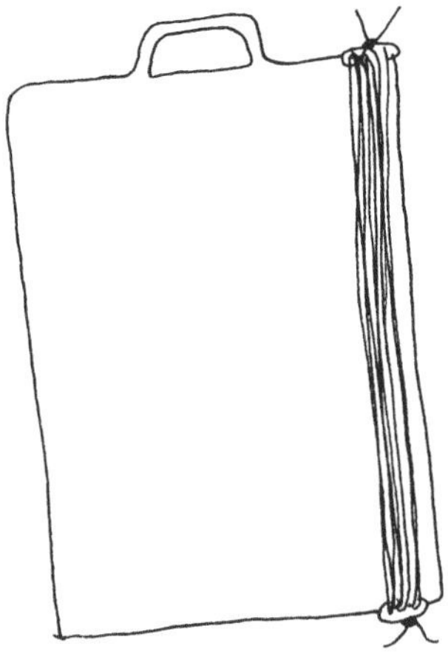

Figure 4.1

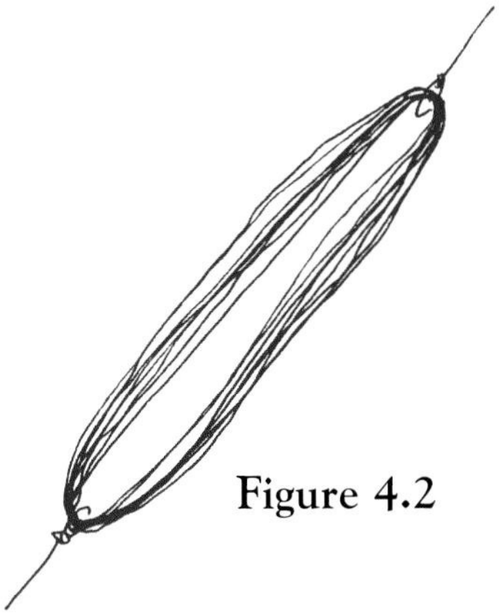

Figure 4.2

2. To remove the thread from the frame, cut two 5-inch pieces of the Fiesta thread, and tie the wrapped thread at either end. (See Fig. 4.1.) Then carefully remove the thread from the frame. Trim away the tied ends.

3. Using wire cutters, cut off the head or eye of the pins. Bend the wire up 1 inch from the bottom. Insert the fiber at the knot. (See Fig. 4.2.) Using pliers, twist the wire around itself. Dab the thread with glue. Add the end cone, pulling it in place over the thread end. (See Fig. 4.3.) Repeat on the other side of the neckpiece. Let the glue dry thoroughly.

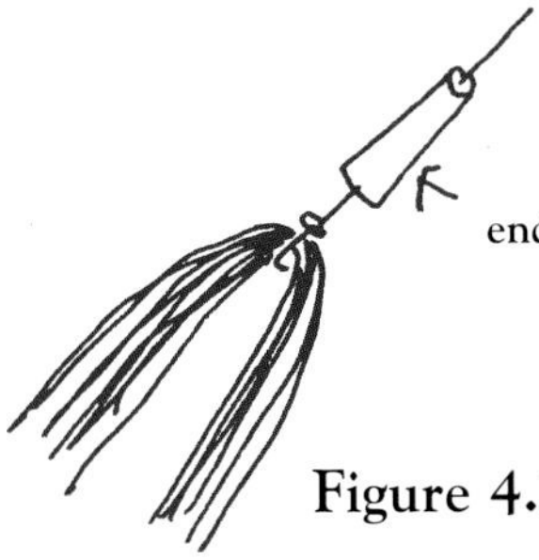

Figure 4.3

4. Grab the end of the wire sticking out of the end cone, and twist it into a loop using the jewelry pliers. (See

Fig. 4.4.) Add a jump ring to the loop. Repeat on the other side. Open the jump rings and add the clasp.

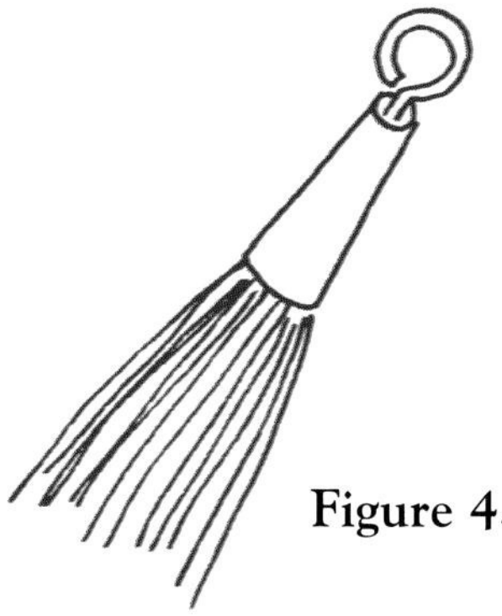

Figure 4.4

5. If you decide to add the optional gold bead, paint the bead with a coat of the sealer, then let it dry thoroughly. Brush the bead with a base coat; let it dry. Next, add two coats of adhesive, allowing the bead to dry between coats. Wrap the gold foil sheet around the bead (matte side to the bead), then remove the foil sheet. Apply the antique finish and wipe off any excess. Then apply the sealer; let it dry. Finally, thread the bead onto the neckpiece, then make an overhand knot on either side of the bead. (See Fig. 4.5.)

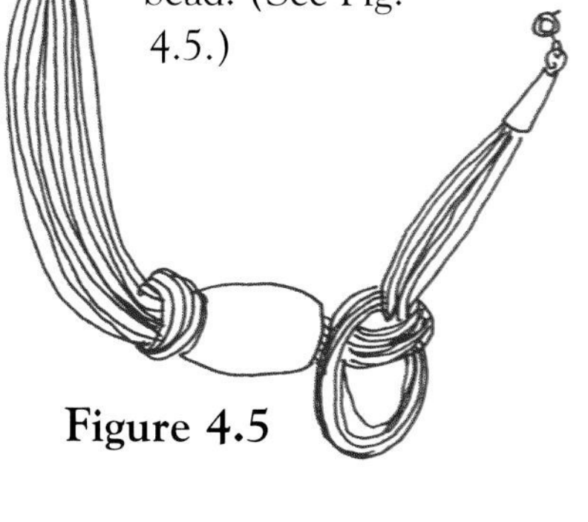

Figure 4.5

ETHNIC MIRRORED PENDANT

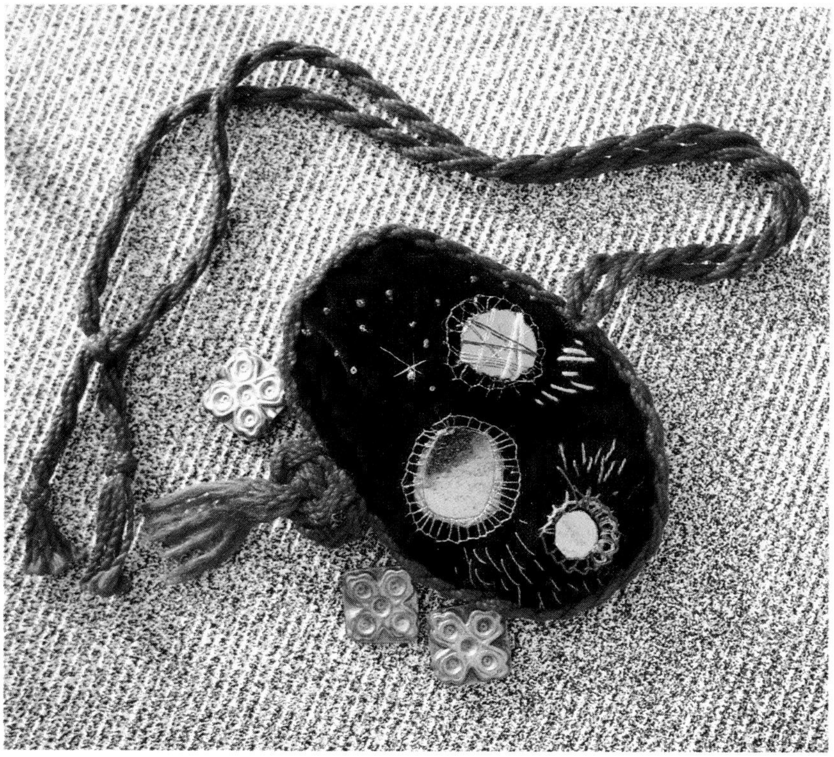

Try your hand at this soft jewelry filled with the incense and intrigue of India. The mirrors, called shi sha, are enhanced with embroidery stitches in vibrant colors, all on a backing of luscious black velvet. This is a good piece for adding your own interpretations. Once you've learned the special techniques involved in making this pendant, let your imagination run wild: Add or delete mirrors, change the background cloth, place embroidery anywhere you like!

Don't stash your beautiful handmade jewelry away in a drawer. Whenever you're not wearing it, use it as wall art. The wall above my desk is filled with jewelry suspended from clear push pins. Display fragile antique pieces under glass.

MATERIALS

Black velvet, 6" × 8" piece
Batting
Shi sha mirrors, one 1" and two ½"
Embroidery floss, regular and metallic
1 cone incense
1 spool pearl cotton, wine-colored
Metal charms (available from TSI, Inc.; see Resources)

TOOLS & SUPPLIES

Tracing paper
Cloth scissors
Roll-on adhesive (optional)
#8 sewing needle
Sewing thread—black, wine
Utility knife

PROCEDURE

1. Trace around the outside oval of Figure 4.6 to make a pattern for this project. Cut out two ovals from the black velvet and one from the batting. Layer one of the velvet pieces right side up on the batting. Set the other velvet piece aside for the backing.

2. While you work, keep mirrors in place with the roll-on adhesive, or you may simply hold the mirror in place. Work the embroidery around the mirror, as shown in Figure 4.7. (This is a good stitch to have in your repertoire, since it

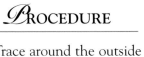

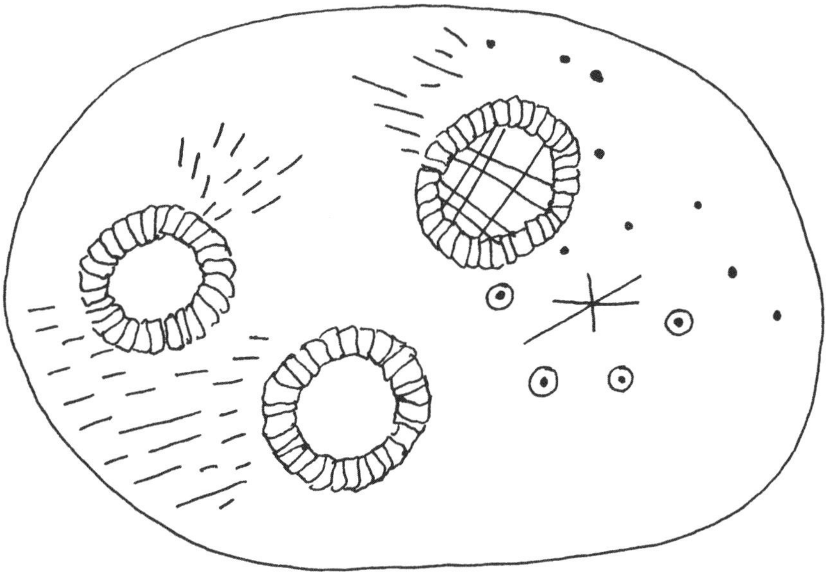

Figure 4.6

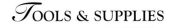

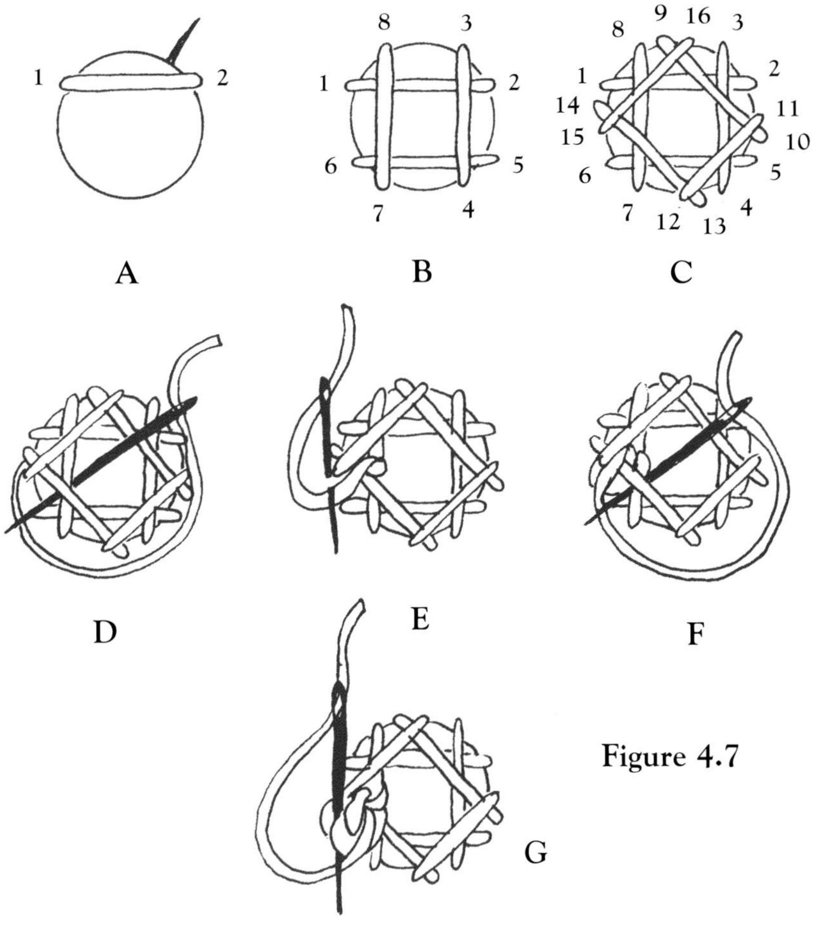

Figure 4.7

can be used to attach any disc shape to cloth.) If you look at the color photograph, you will notice I have taken liberties with the stitch and worked some of the threads directly across the mirror. Feel free to experiment.

3. Add more embroidery around the mirrors using the stitches shown in Figures 4.8 and 4.9.

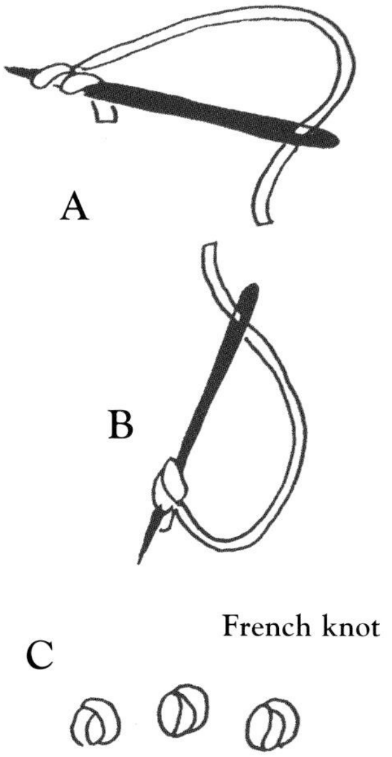

Figure 4.8

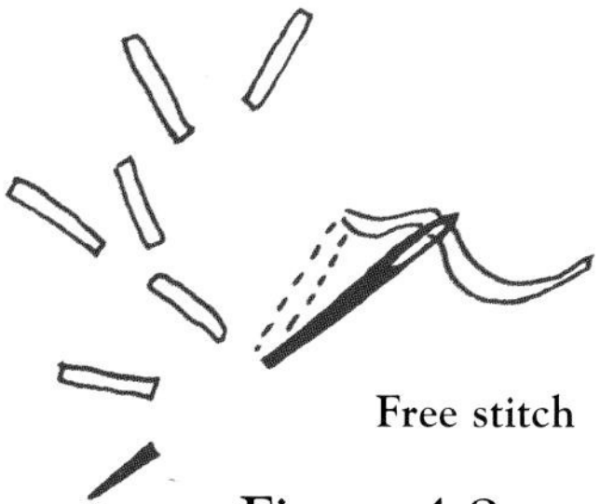

Figure 4.9

4. Place the black velvet backing piece right side down on the embellished velvet oval. Sew around ¼ inch from the outside edge, leaving a 2-inch opening for turning. Turn the piece right side out. Shave a bit of the incense onto the batting. Turn the raw edge to the inside and whipstitch the opening to close it.

5. Monk's cord is made by winding thin cord upon itself to create a thicker, more substantial cord. This procedure is easier if another person is holding the other end: Take a 6-foot length of the pearl cotton and fold it in half once. With each person holding an end, twirl the cord in opposite directions until it starts to wrap upon itself. Then fold the cord in half again, and let go of the end—the cord will retain its shape. Couch the cord around the outside edge of the velvet pendant. Fashion the remaining cord into a fancy twist. (See Fig. 4.10.)

Figure 4.10

6. Cut a 12-foot length of the pearl cotton. Make it into monk's cord. Find the center of the cord and sew it to the top of the pendant. Tie the ends of the cord closed with an overhand knot. Trim the ends, then tie both cords together.

7. Sew the charms in place at the bottom edge of the pendant.

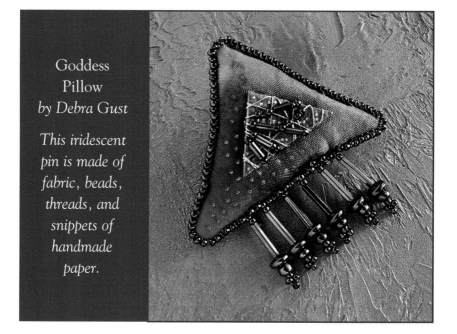

Goddess Pillow *by Debra Gust*

This iridescent pin is made of fabric, beads, threads, and snippets of handmade paper.

WOOD PROJECTS

FLOATING WOOD NECKLACE

Since you can't see the hanging cord on this necklace (it's monofilament nylon thread), the pieces of wood seem to float magically around the neck. Using a special threading technique, you can move the beads into new positions on a whim. Although the wood beads used here are slices of coconut shell that have been dyed a dark teal-green, the "floating" design would work with other beads as well.

Materials

Transparent (monofilament nylon) thread or fishing line
Clear pony beads
Wooden coconut shell beads in graduated sizes
Screw clasp without end loops

Tools & Supplies

Scissors
#8 sewing needle
BOND 527 cement

Procedure

1. Plan your graduated design on paper. This necklace is made of two strands: The top strand finishes at 16 inches with 11 bead clusters. The bottom strand finishes at 22 inches with 17 bead clusters.

2. Cut two pieces of transparent thread: one 22 inches long and the other 28 inches long. It doesn't matter whether you work the short or the long strand first, since both are constructed the same way.

3. Thread the needle, then string on 1 pony bead, 1 wood bead, and 1 pony bead. Insert the needle back through the wood piece and the first pony bead. (See Fig. 4.11.) Use this same technique to add as many bead clusters as you like. Be sure to leave at least 3 inches of thread at the end of each strand for attaching the clasp.

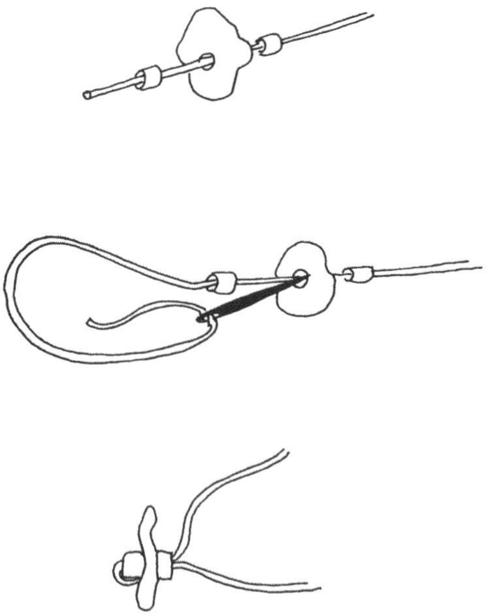

Figure 4.11

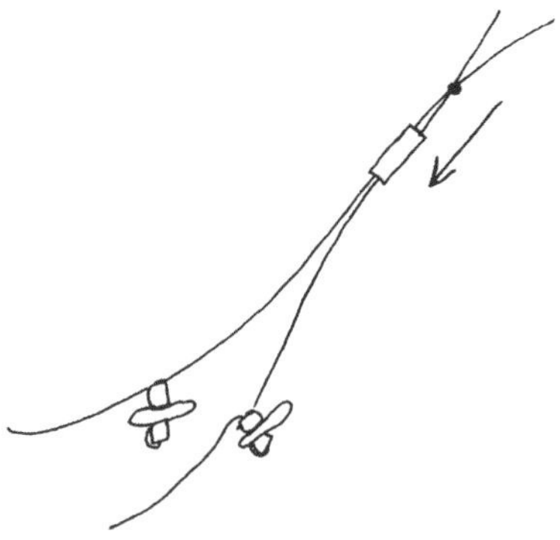

Figure 4.12

4. Thread each strand end into the screw clasp. (See Fig. 4.12.) Tie the ends in a square knot and clip away the excess thread. Pull the knot down into the clasp, then dot with glue. Repeat for the other end of the necklace.

> Always buy long (3-inch) head pins. They are more versatile & you can fashion any leftover pieces into eye pins using your jewelry pliers.

REVERSIBLE WOOD WHIMSY

Transform a plain piece of wood into a double-faced necklace with a few brush strokes and a passel of beads. For best results, use Deka Gloss paint—it's specially formulated for use on wood and doesn't need a sealer.

MATERIALS

Block of wood, 1⅛" square
4 white round wooden beads, 8mm
1 string yellow wooden beads, 6mm
2 wooden tube beads, ¾" long
Small eye screw
1 spool transparent thread

TOOLS & SUPPLIES

Sandpaper
Cloth (for wiping the wood)
Tracing paper
Deka Gloss paint—blue, black, white, yellow
Paintbrushes—liner and #6 round
Water jar (for rinsing brushes)
Heavy wire, 6" long
Pushpins
Ruler
#8 sharp sewing needle

PROCEDURE

1. Sand the wooden block to smooth the edges. Wipe the block with a clean cloth to remove dust. Trace the patterns shown in Figure 4.13, and transfer them onto each side of the wooden block.

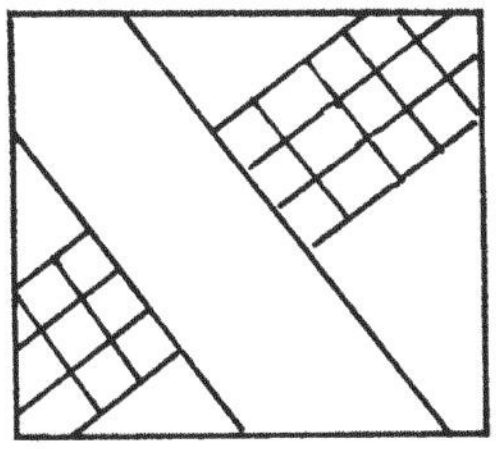

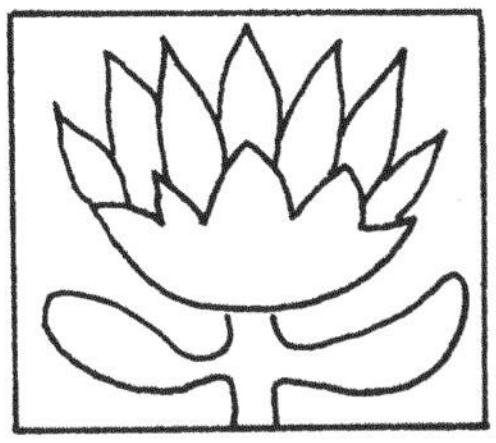

Figure 4.13

2. Paint one side of the block, then let it dry. Repeat for the other side of the block. Use the liner brush for very small areas and the #6 brush for larger areas. Use the color photograph as a guide for colors or experiment with your own color scheme. Paint the edges of the block with blue paint; let it dry.

3. String 3 of the medium-sized white beads on the wire. Wind the ends of the wire around a pushpin, and stick them on the edge of a shelf. (See Fig. 4.14.) (This arrangement allows you to paint the beads fully in one step.) Paint all of the white beads solid black. Let them dry, then paint white dots on one of the black beads. Allow it to dry, then remove the beads from the wire. String 16 yellow beads on the wire. Paint them black, let them dry, then remove them.

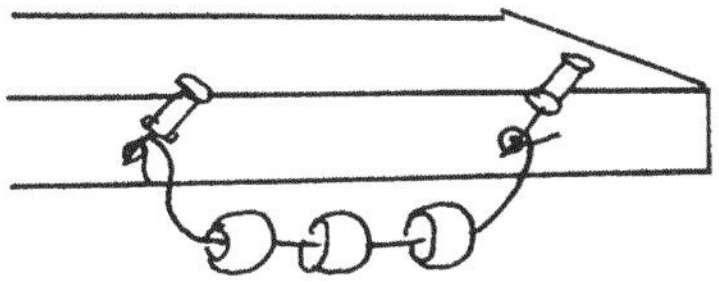

Figure 4.14

4. String the two tube beads on the wire; suspend them from a shelf. Using the liner brush, dot the beads with many blue circles and a few yellow circles.

5. Measure the top of the wooden block. Insert the eye screw in the middle, then paint it black.

6. Cut a length of thread 30 inches long. Find the center of the thread and insert it through the eye screw. Make a loop, then bring the ends of the thread through the loop and tighten. (See Fig. 4.15.)

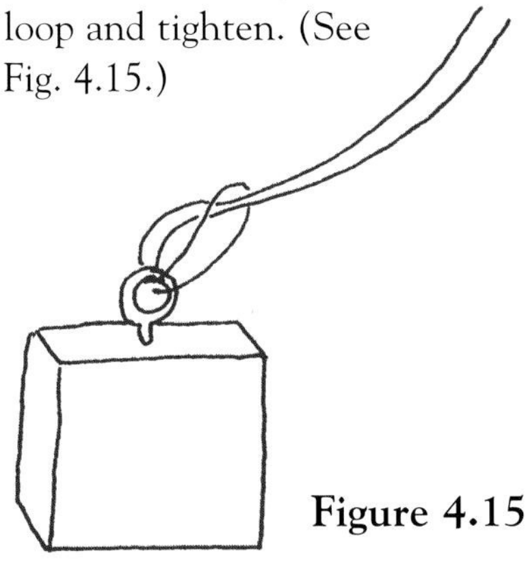

Figure 4.15

7. Starting on the right-hand side, string 4 yellow beads, 1 medium-size black bead, 8 yellow beads, 1 tube bead, 65 yellow beads (or 8½ inches), 1 medium-sized white bead with dots, and 1 small black bead. Put the needle on the thread

Figure 4.16

end, and go back through the dotted bead. (See Fig. 4.16.) Knot the thread to the strung thread, then run it back through 6 or 8 of the strung beads. Clip off the excess thread.

8. For the left side, string 4 yellow beads, 1 medium-sized black bead, 8 yellow beads, 1 tube bead, 65 yellow beads (or 8½ inches), 1 black medium-sized bead, and 15 small black beads. Slip the needle on the working thread, and insert the needle through the first small black bead (this forms a loop of beads) and through the black bead. (See Fig. 4.17.) Knot the working thread to the strung bead thread. Insert the needle back through 6 or 8 of the strung yellow beads. Cut off the excess thread.

9. Decide which side of the wood block you wish to display (Modern Abstract or Perky Sunflower), then place the dotted black bead through the loop of beads. The weight of the piece will hold the necklace in place.

Figure 4.17

Untitled by Maxine Peretz Prange

This multistrand necklace uses beads of many different materials. Strands separate and join along the length of the necklace. It is strung on waxed linen with a wrapped loop and bead closure.

PAPER PROJECTS

WATERCOLOR & JEWEL EARRINGS

Painting is so powerful—one swipe of a paint-loaded brush, and the paper is transformed. For this pair of earrings, you'll be using a simple "wet-in-wet" technique, which makes the paint flow and mingle with little work from you. It's magic!

MATERIALS

90# watercolor paper, 18" × 10" sheet

Watercolor paint—colors of your choice (I used alizarin crimson and hunter green)

2 small purple rhinestones with silver settings

1 pair flat pad post-style studs with earring nuts

6 seed bead pearls, size 11

TOOLS & SUPPLIES

Masking tape

Paintbrush

Water jar (for rinsing brush)

Tracing paper

Scissors or utility knife

Paper punch

White glue

Large pin

Acrylic medium, gloss (available at art-supply centers)

PROCEDURE

1. Wet the watercolor paper with water. Hold the paper by the corner to allow excess water to drain away. Place the paper on the work surface and tape it in place. This step, called "stretching" the paper, prevents wrinkles, gullies, and waves from appearing on the paper's surface.

2. Load the brush with paint and draw it across the wet paper. Rinse the brush, then add paint of a different color and allow the colors to mingle. For example, use blue paint, then add a bit of red nearby; a purple color will appear where the two colors merge. (When mixing colors for this project, keep in mind the fundamentals: Red and yellow produce orange; red and blue make purple; and yellow and blue create green. For further guidance, consult color mixing charts, available at art-supply stores.) Once the paper is painted, allow it to dry thoroughly.

3. Trace the triangle shown in Figure 4.18. Look at the watercolor painting, select an area to use for the earrings, then cut out the triangles. Also, cut two strips measuring 1½ inches by ⅛ inch. Using the paper punch, cut out eight "dots" of leftover watercolor paper.

4. Using Figure 4.19 or the color photo as a guide for placement, poke the rhinestone settings through the back side of the paper triangles. Set the rhinestones in place; push down the prongs to secure the stones. Glue the paper strips in place, then glue the "dots" in place. Let everything dry.

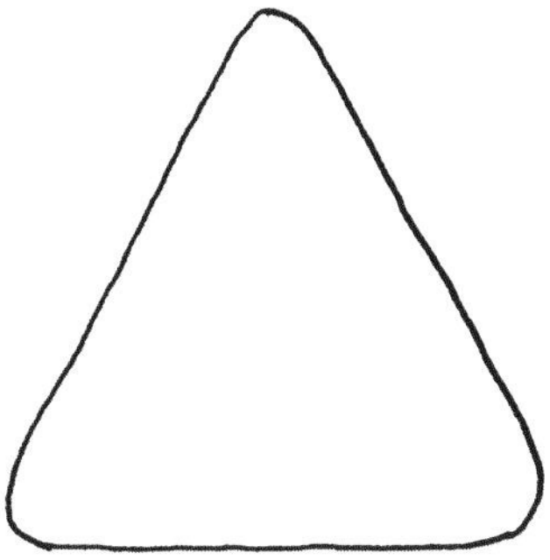

Figure 4.18

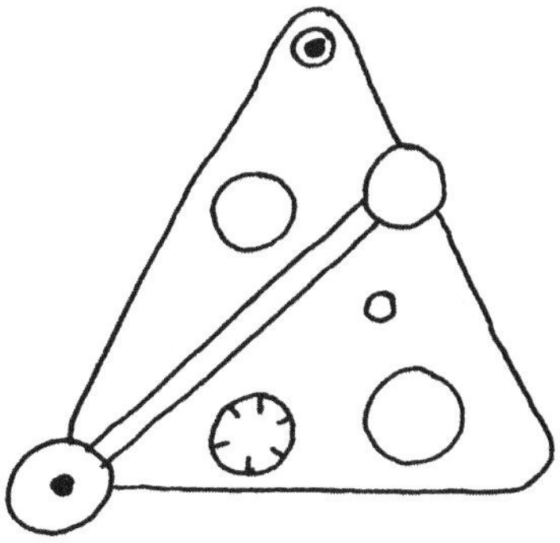

Figure 4.19

5. Use the large pin to make a pilot hole at the top of the triangle for each earring. Dab the holes with glue. Insert the earring posts through the holes, then glue on the seed pearls. Allow the glue to dry.

6. Using a clean paintbrush and glossy acrylic medium, glaze the earrings. (Be careful to avoid the rhinestones.) Let the glaze dry. Place the earring nuts on the posts.

ORIGAMI-STYLE PAINTED EARRINGS

Hand-paint a unique pair of earrings with the look of origami, the Japanese art of paper folding. For a different look, use some of the luscious handmade papers.

MATERIALS

90# watercolor paper, 18" × 10" sheet
Watercolor paint set
Silver metallic decorative tape, ½" wide
1 pair silver kidney ear wires
2 silver beads, size 11

TOOLS & SUPPLIES

Masking tape
Paintbrushes
Water jar (for rinsing brushes)
Paper towel
Tracing paper
Utility knife
White glue
Large needle
Polymer medium, gloss

PROCEDURE

1. "Stretch" the watercolor paper by soaking it in tepid water, letting the water drain away, then taping the paper to the work surface with masking tape.

2. Load the brush with lots of water, dip it in paint, then skim the brush across the paper. Rinse and dry off the brush with a paper towel before adding another color. Experiment with the paint: Paint some areas solid, use the tip of the brush to make dots, or tap a loaded brush to create a spattered effect. Fill the entire sheet with interesting designs and colors, then let it dry thoroughly.

3. Trace the large triangle pattern shown in Figure 4.20, and cut it out using the utility knife. Select an area on the watercolor sheet for the earrings, then cut them out. Remember, the earrings don't have to match exactly. If you use areas of the watercolor paper that have the same colors, your earrings will have a coordinated look.

4. Lightly transfer the placement lines for the metallic strips. Use pieces of tape that are slightly longer than the pattern so that you can wrap the ends around to the back of the triangles to create a nice, clean edge. Attach the tape firmly.

5. Using the small triangle pattern shown in Figure 4.20, cut two pieces of the watercolor paper that have a solid color, or some other area that will contrast with the large triangles. Set these pieces aside.

6. Fold the large triangles on the dotted lines toward the unpainted side. Open them up, then coat the inside with glue. Before closing them completely, slip the small accent triangles partly under one cut edge. (See the color photograph for placement.) Let the glue dry.

7. Using a large needle, make a hole at the top of each earring. Place a kidney wire through each hole, then slip on a small bead as a finishing ornament.

8. Coat the earrings with gloss polymer medium. (Avoid the metallic strips.) Let them dry thoroughly.

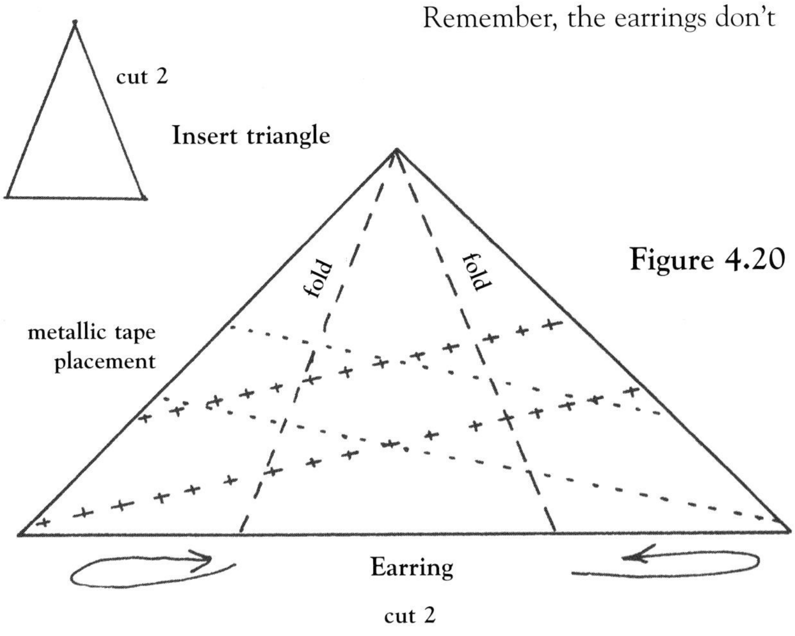

Figure 4.20

CHAPTER 5

STYLISH NOVELTIES

Using Natural & Man-made Found Objects

Sometimes the most beautiful materials are found literally at one's feet, just waiting to be picked up—for instance, gorgeous seashells seen during a long walk on the beach or interesting rocks discovered while at a mountain retreat. Don't overlook curious objects you unearth at antique shops, the dollar stores, and the like. Have fun hunting!

SHELL PROJECTS

SLEEK SEASHELL STICK PIN WITH GOLDEN FRINGE

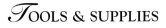

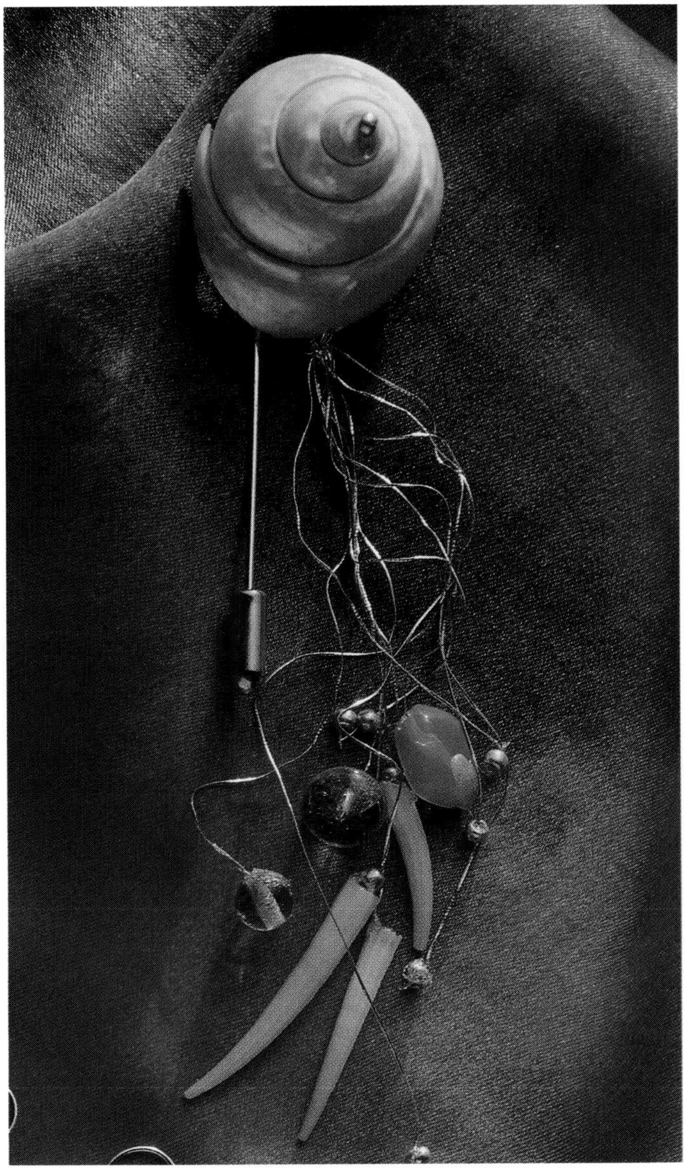

One beautiful shell was the inspiration for this design. Consisting of a gold stick pin with an array of beads and shells dangling from slinky gold threads, this piece is both interesting and good-looking.

MATERIALS

Pearl moon shell, or any other large shell
Goldtone stick pin
Madeira gold thread
10 gold metal seed beads, size 11
3 small tusk shells
3 assorted blue glass beads

TOOLS & SUPPLIES

Electric drill with fine bit
Bond 527 cement
Scissors

PROCEDURE

1. Lay the moon shell in place on the stick pin. Mark a hole on the side of the shell for attaching the fringe. (See Fig. 5.0.) Drill the hole with a fine bit at high speed so the shell doesn't break. Glue

the moon shell to the stick pin. Let it dry for 24 hours.

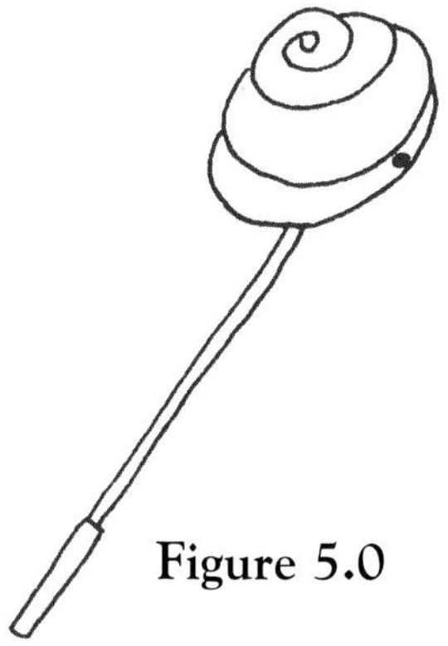

Figure 5.0

2. Cut six pieces of gold thread ranging from 10 to 12 inches in length. Insert the threads through the hole on the side of the shell, and tie in an overhand knot. (See Fig. 5.1.) One by one, dip each thread end into the glue and add an attachment (gold bead, gold bead and tusk shell, or blue glass bead). Add 3 blue glass beads, 3 tusk shells each with a gold bead, and 6 gold beads on the 12 thread ends. Allow all of the glued attachments to dry thoroughly without touching one another. Glue a gold bead to the point of the large shell you are using, if the shell will accommodate it. Let the glue dry.

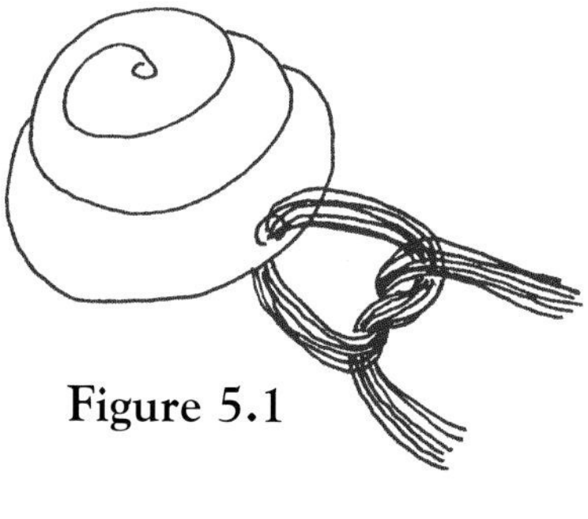

Figure 5.1

GIFT-OF-THE-SEA PIN

The exquisite turret shell is the centerpiece of this pin. Bits of ocean-colored lace, a symphony of beads, and wisps of silver metallic threads are added to enhance the shell's subtle beauty.

MATERIALS

Turret shell, or any other long shell (e.g., cerith, wentletrap, or auger)

Scrap of variegated lace in blues, purples, and greens (or any unique piece of lace in marine colors)

Circle pin back, 24mm

Madeira silver metallic thread

Faux white, purple, and champagne-colored pearl beads

Gold beads, size 8

TOOLS & SUPPLIES

Scissors

GOOP adhesive

PROCEDURE

1. Cut a piece of lace 5½ inches square. Gather the middle of the piece into small pleats. (See Fig. 5.2a.) Dab a bit of glue onto the pin back. Add another dab of glue onto the middle of the lace where it is gathered, then place the lace on the pin back. (See Fig. 5.2b.) Add more glue to the back top edge of the shell and place it on the lace.

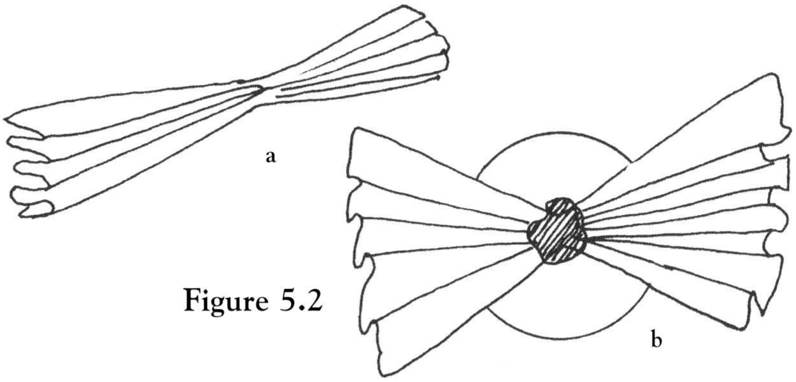

Figure 5.2

2. Dab a bit of glue on the shell opening. Wind a 12-inch length of silver thread around two fingers. (See Fig. 5.3.) Carefully remove the threads and place them in the shell opening so that the thread ends stand above the opening. (See Fig. 5.4.)

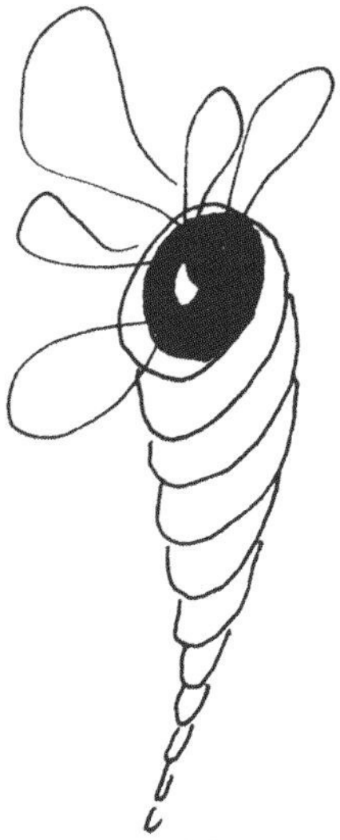

Figure 5.4

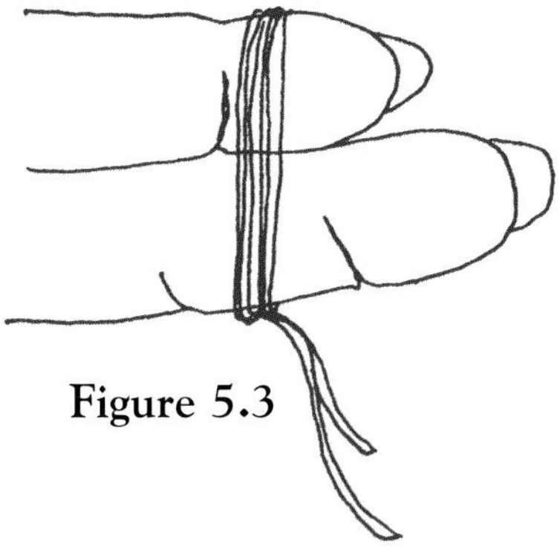

Figure 5.3

3. Glue a large pearl bead into the shell opening, as shown in Fig. 5.4, then fill in with more beads. (See the color photograph; I used 12 faux pearl shells and 3 gold beads.) Let the piece dry.

> Remember, gold & silver can be used effectively together in the same piece to give it a sophisticated look. Also, a piece doesn't necessarily need to be symmetrical in design. Use off-center designs to create visual interest.

MAN-MADE TREASURES PROJECTS

ANTIQUE COBALT VIAL WITH BEADED CROCHET CORD

MATERIALS

Focal point treasure

Pearl cotton, in a color to complement your treasure (I used tan thread wrapped with gold thread)

Beads for embellishing neck cord (I used 28 shell-style beads for the neck cord and 2 for the dangle)

Dangle adornments—beads, charms, unusual buttons

Shank-style button, ¾", for closure

TOOLS & SUPPLIES

Scissors

Crochet hook, size H

PROCEDURE

1. Plan your design on paper if it deviates from the design shown. Create a focal point, then plot out further embellishment, including any dangling adornments you wish to use. (See Fig. 5.5 for examples.) In the design shown the shell-shaped beads are attached closer together near the focal point; they are spaced farther apart as the hanging cord progresses to the closure. The extra embellishment adds interest to the focal point piece; it also adds movement to the piece.

As you plan your design, remember that the hole on any attachments should be large enough to accommodate a doubled strand of pearl cotton. Also, keep in mind that the closure is simply decorative and does not open, so don't make the cord shorter than the prescribed length, or it won't fit over your head.

Once you've laid out your design, you're ready to begin construction. Trust your instincts—your design will be wonderful.

2. Working directly off the spool of pearl cotton, make a small loop (large enough to insert the crochet hook), and tie a knot. Then follow the steps shown in Figure 5.6 for "chaining":

a. Insert the hook through the loop, pick up a strand of pearl cotton, then bring it up through the loop. Continue in this manner, creating a chain of loops.

b. Anytime you wish to add an attachment (bead or but-

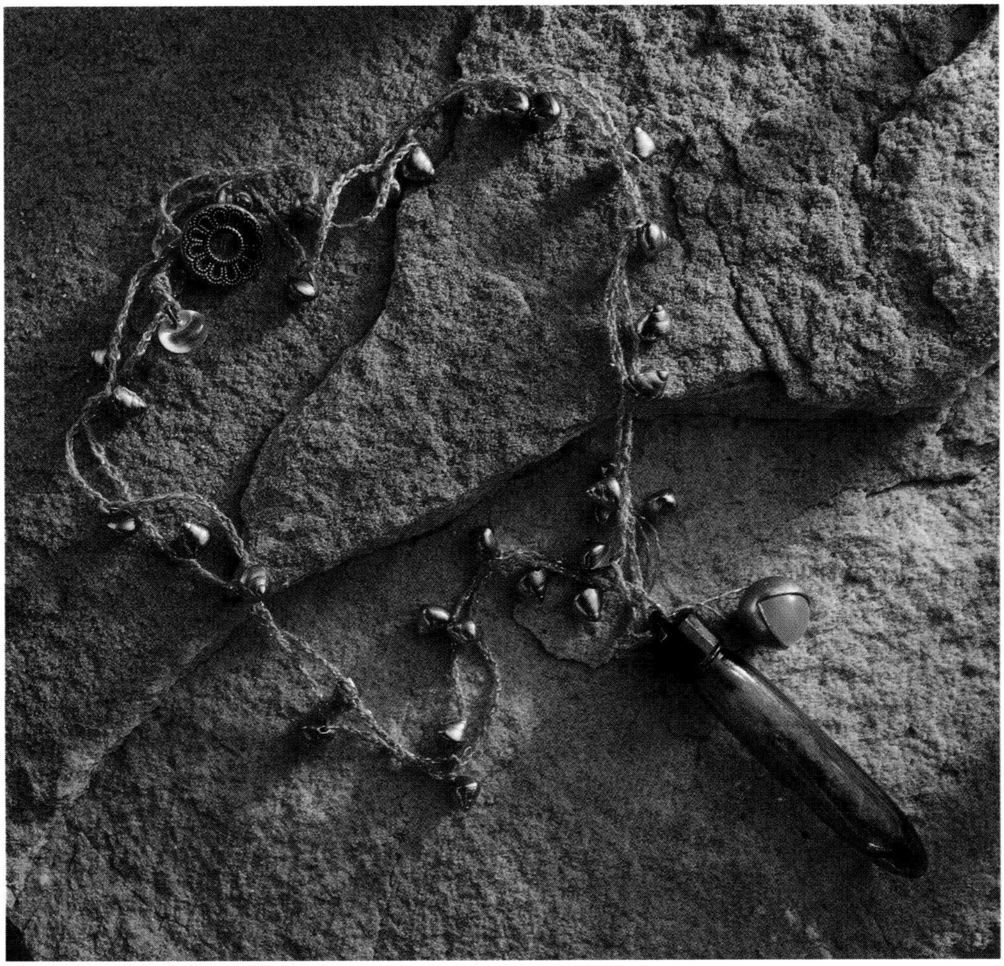

Look for interesting perfume bottles, unique charms—basically anything intriguing that can be attached to a hanging cord. This is sure to be a one-of-a-kind piece!

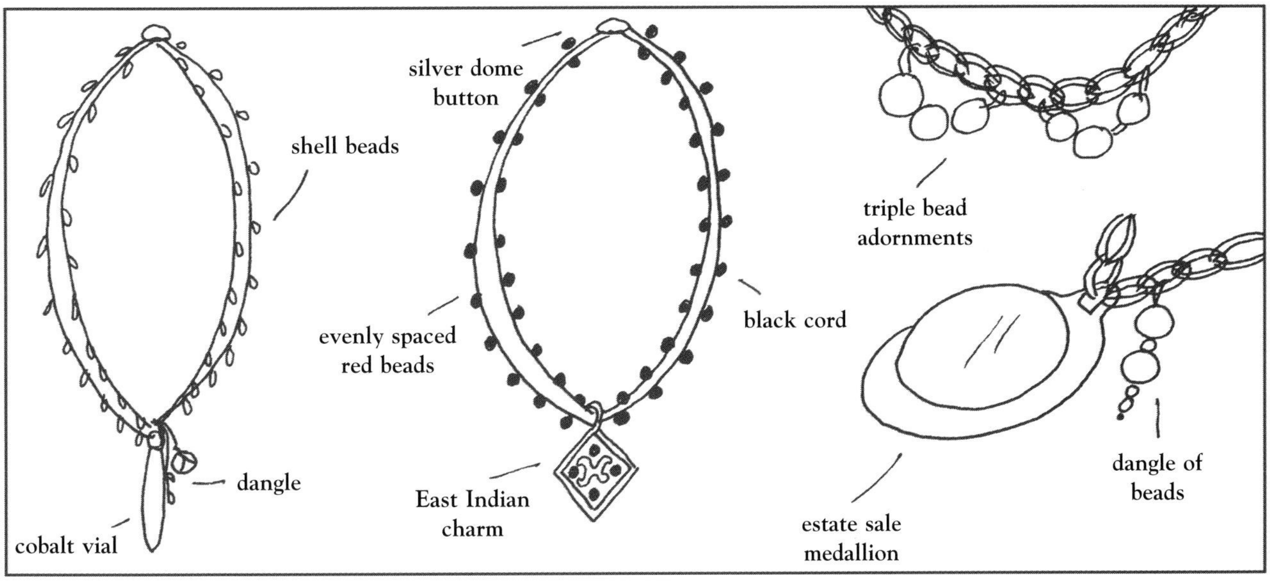

Figure 5.5

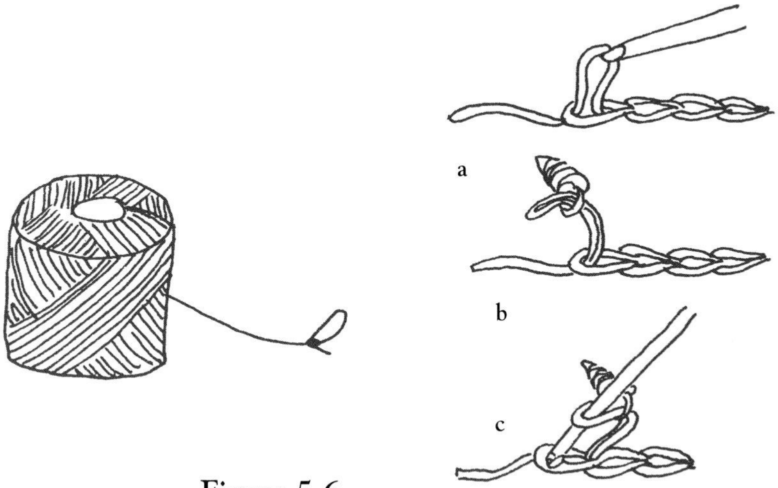

Figure 5.6

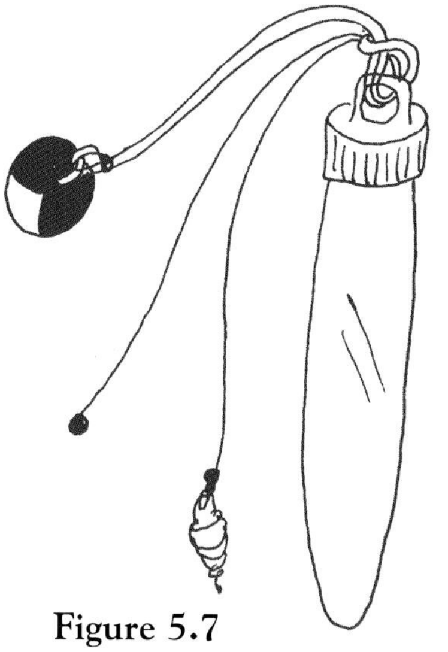

Figure 5.7

ton), remove the hook and insert the loop of pearl cotton through the hole on the attachment.

C. Replace the hook through the loop, then pull through the previous chain loop.

3. To create a piece like the one shown, work a 13-inch length of chaining, adding attachments whenever you like. Add the focal point, then continue chaining and adding attachments for another 13 inches. Add on a shank-style button. Chain for 2 more inches, then tie on a small decorative button to end the chain. (You can also add another dangle here, if you like.) Tie the beginning end of the crochet cord under the large shank-style button.

4. To create the focal point embellishment, take an 8-inch-long piece of pearl cotton and insert it through the hole on the focal point piece. Add on a decorative button or bead, then stick the thread end back through the hole. (See Fig. 5.7.) Tie a knot in the cords, then tie a bead onto each thread end.

Untitled
by Freya Ellinwood

This 26-inch necklace is made of 4mm black glass beads, Tuareg brass beads, and bone beads collected in Mali. The 2-inch carved conus shell "Hippo Tooth" centerpiece was collected in Cote D'Ivoire.

Rhythm in art has to do with the movement of line in a given space; the contrasting design, for example, of straight lines and curves, highs and lows, ins and outs. The rhythms you design can lead the viewer's eye in a visual tempo of your own making, as lyrical as a Debussy piano movement or as strong and intense as a Wagnerian opera. Just as you feel rhythm in music and dance, often to the point of moving your body to its engaging patterns, so will you feel rhythm in the emerging sculptural forms of your imagination.

Judith Peck
Sculpture as Experience

8 LOEW — CORNELL 7300
SHADER
JAPAN

PART TWO

ACCESSORIES

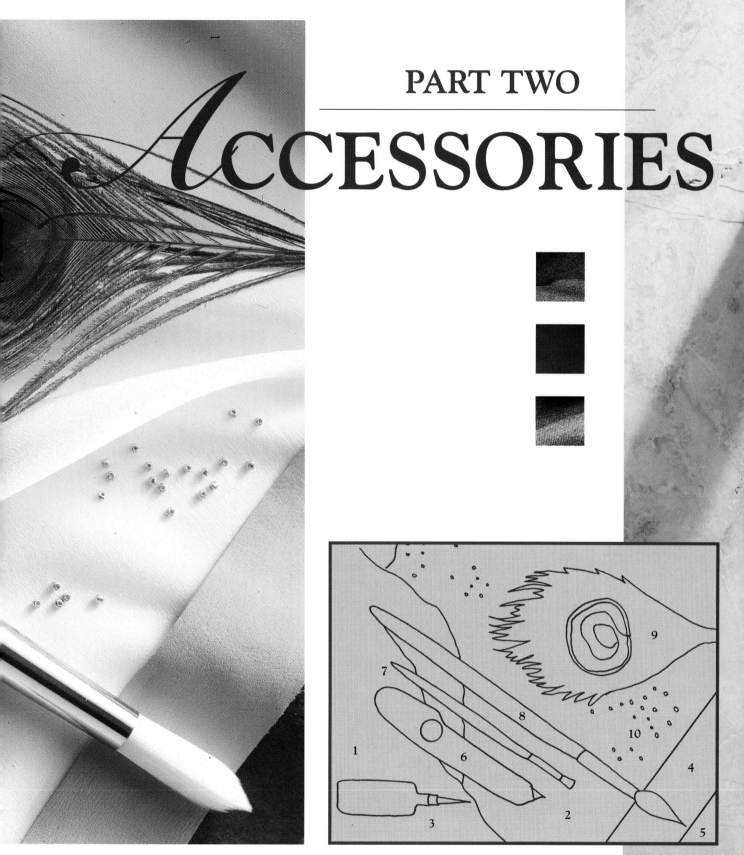

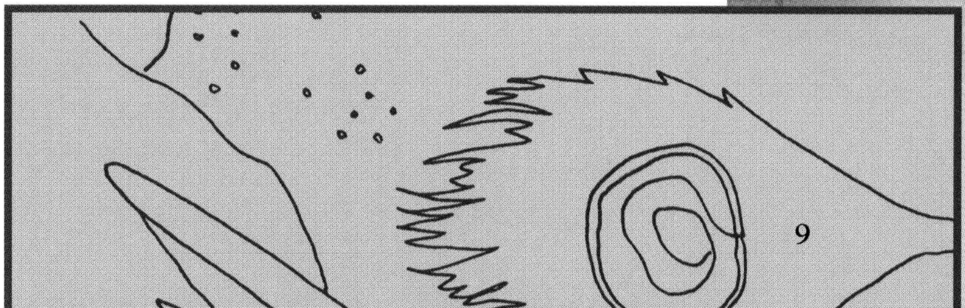

1. *Crepe de chine silk* **2.** *China silk* **3.** *Applicator bottle with fine tip* **4.** *Soft leather*
5. *Wool felt* **6.** *Utility knife* **7.** *#8 flat paintbrush* **8.** *#12 round paintbrush*
9. *Peacock feather* **10.** *Metal seed beads, size 8*

CHAPTER 6

ACCESSORIES MATERIALS

The Finest Goods

One fine way to create your own signature style is to use distinctive accessories, such as belts, hats, scarves, and bags. I've designed a collection using the finest materials—rich, cascading silks; buttery, soft leather; handsome hand-dyed cottons; exotic peacock feathers; fine wool felt; and delicate millinery veiling shot through with golden lamé threads.

Although most of these materials are usually thought of as fancy and "after-five," I've brought them out for everyday use. These accessories, which you can adapt to your own unique tastes, are meant to be enjoyed anytime.

All accessories transform a ho-hum wardrobe into something special. Simply put, accessories make you feel good. I can't think of a better reason for you to try some of the projects and techniques in this section.

Silk

Silk may be textured or absolutely smooth and is available in a variety of colors. White silk is the easiest to find and the best to work on, at least in the beginning. After you have developed a good sense of the way colors blend and have investigated all the different silk-painting techniques, then you can branch out into the colored silks.

Silk also comes in various weights. These are designated by the double-m symbol "mm," which stands for "mommie" (pronounced "mummy"). The 8mm is the most popular and readily available weight for silk scarves. You can purchase either silk by the yard or hand-hemmed scarf blanks in both rectangles and squares.

Please note that most silks have small imperfections. This is natural and acceptable.

STANDARD SCARF SIZES

Use these measurements to plan your own projects.

Squares

8" to 54" square

Rectangles

25" × 25"

11" × 60"

35" × 35"

14" × 72"

45" × 45"

Handkerchiefs

11" × 11"

16" × 16"

Sarong

45" × 72"

TYPES OF SILK

Habotai or China silk is available in a 5mm to 10mm weight. It has a luster finish that enhances the colors and is a good choice for beginners.

Silk georgette (8mm) has a slight texture. Try using it for long, filmy scarves. Crepe de chine (14mm to 16mm) is another beautiful silk with a slightly pebbly texture. It works up nicely into beautiful clothing or scarves, and the added weight gives it a very posh look and feel.

Silk charmeuse is a crepe-backed silk satin. One side is very slick and smooth; the other has a soft, crepey texture. Use a 20mm weight for clothing and heavier scarves. Some suppliers carry a lighter weight for finer scarves.

Pongee silk is a lighter weight (12mm or so) and can be used for scarves if you pretreat it with a special softener available from mail-order suppliers. Silk duppioni and silk shantung are quite textural, with tiny slubs throughout the weave. These silks are usually used for clothing.

CARING FOR SILK

Silk can be dry-cleaned or washed by hand. Hand-wash the silk gently in tepid water using a mild shampoo; do not overagitate. Rinse thoroughly in tepid water until the water runs clear. (As you rinse, you can add a little vinegar, which removes soap residue and sets color.) Lay the silk on a large towel, then roll the towel to absorb most of the moisture. Lay the silk over a rod and let it dry.

Beware of commercial cleaners touted as specifically formulated for fine washables—some of them actually pull color out of fabric. Test any cleaner before you use it. Since silk is a natural fabric, I prefer to use a very mild shampoo. Just be sure to rinse thoroughly to rid the material of any residue.

Once you have hand-washed silk, always hand-wash it. If your silk has been dry-cleaned, be careful not to get water on it, or permanent spotting may occur.

PAINTING SILK SCARVES

Hand-painted silk scarves are one of the most indulgent accessories you can make for yourself. They give an air of ambience and accent your beauty whenever you wear them.

The colors used on the scarves in the color photograph really aren't paints—they're dyes. Paint lies on top of the surface and is absorbed a bit into the cloth. Dyes, on the other hand, actually penetrate each strand of the cloth fibers. This absorption of color is particularly important with scarves where both sides will show. Dyes also offer more brilliant color retention. Jacquard and Deka are two excellent brands of silk color.

RESISTS

Resists are substances used to prevent the dye from being absorbed into the cloth fibers. Whenever you want to create a motif that is distinct from the background, you use a resist. Any silk scarf with representational shapes that you can readily identify—for example, a cat, bird, or geometric shape—was made with a resist.

For the painted silk project called Chasing Butterflies, I use a traditional gutta resist. Gutta resists are also available in colors. Some are water-soluble; others must be removed by dry-cleaning.

Wax warmed to a liquid can be applied with a brush or with the traditional tjanting used in batik. (See Fig. 6.1.) You can crack the wax to achieve the traditional crazed appearance of batik (by gathering and rumpling the fabric), or you can simply use it as a resist. To remove the wax, iron the silk between sheets of absorbent paper.

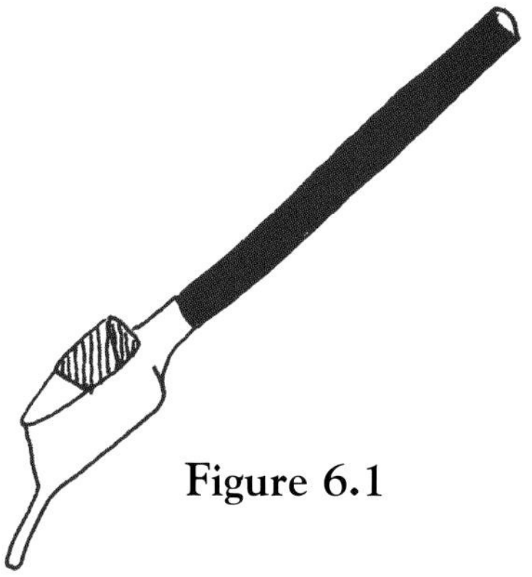

Figure 6.1

Regardless of the type of resist you choose, the general way it is used—that is, to outline a shape—is the same. Like motifs designed for stenciling work, the motifs used with resists should be closed shapes. (See Fig. 6.2.) You can also use resists to create open-ended linear shapes. (See Fig. 6.3.)

SPECIAL EFFECTS

Both salt and sugar can be used to create atmospheric effects.

When you sprinkle salt on wet silk paint, each granule absorbs some of the color, resulting in starbursts with a textural quality. Kosher salt

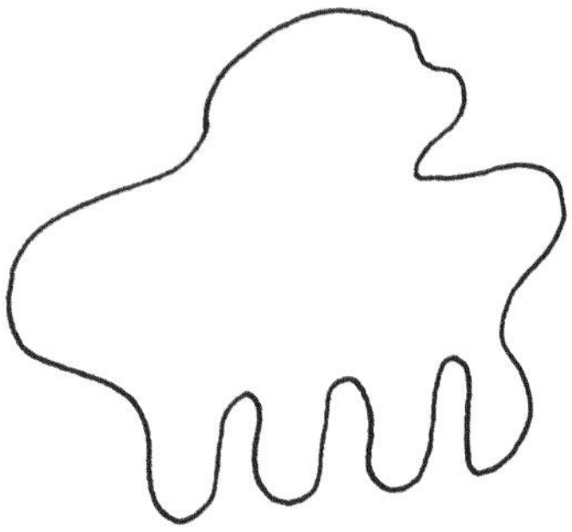

Figure 6.2

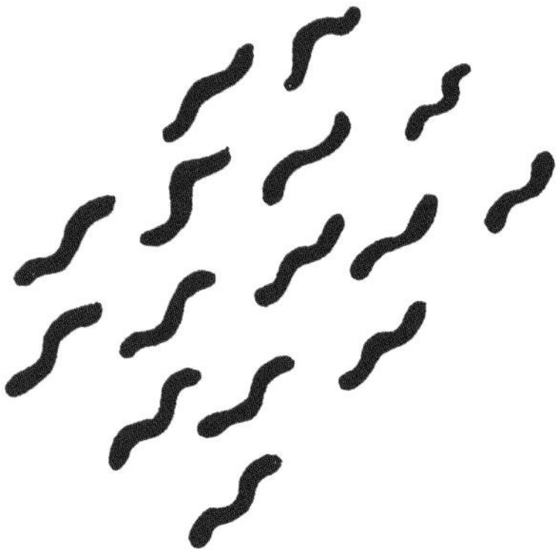

Figure 6.3

works fine; common table salt gives a more subtle effect. Some of the silk color suppliers carry salt specifically for this purpose.

I first learned of the sugar technique in an excellent book, *Silk Painting,* by Jill Kennedy and Jane Varrall (Chilton, 1991). The authors use a sugar syrup (sugar mixed with warm water) and drizzle it down the length of the silk—thick in spots, thin in others—to create a streaked pattern.

The sugar syrup is so thick, the silk takes at least three days to dry here in the Midwest, where I live, during a humid summer. So far, the results have been mixed, but I plan to try this technique again during the winter, when the humidity plummets. Although silk is one of the strongest materials available, I feel I have compromised the silk by leaving it wet for so long. Consult *Silk Painting* for detailed instructions on how to use this special technique.

FRAMES

When you color silk, including silk scarves, the silk must be attached to a frame and suspended above the work surface so that the color doesn't run into areas you don't want it to. (An exception is the rainbow watercolor technique, which was used to make the scarf pictured on the cover and is explained at the end of the Monet's Rose Garden project in Chapter 7.) In general, the best way to paint any silk scarf is to first stretch the silk on a frame.

You can make a frame with artist's stretcher bars. These wooden bars are sold in pairs at art-supply stores. (For example, if you wanted a frame measuring 30 inches by 36 inches, you would buy a pair of 30-inch bars and a pair of 36-inch bars.) The bar frames are easy to construct—just slide them together at the corners, then brace them with a small chink of wood. The disadvantage of this type of frame is that its size is not adjustable.

If you plan to make many scarves in different sizes, I would suggest you invest in an adjustable fabric frame, available from suppliers that sell silk-painting supplies. Cerulean Blue, Ltd., offers a pine frame that can be adjusted from 2 inches all the way up to 48 inches by 60 inches. This special frame allows you to make both rectangular and square scarves.

Of course, if you are handy with wood, or know someone who is, you can make your own frame from standard lumber. My husband took time off from creating fantasy furniture to make me a 14-by-72-inch painting frame out of two-by-fours. As

> **UTILITY KNIVES**
>
> X-acto makes handy knives in a variety of styles and shapes. Keep a supply of new blades handy, or resharpen blades with a whetstone. Hone the blade by moving it in a circular motion, then wipe it off before using.
>
> The knife in the color photograph at the beginning of this chapter contains six blades. When one blade gets dull, you simply snap it off and continue.

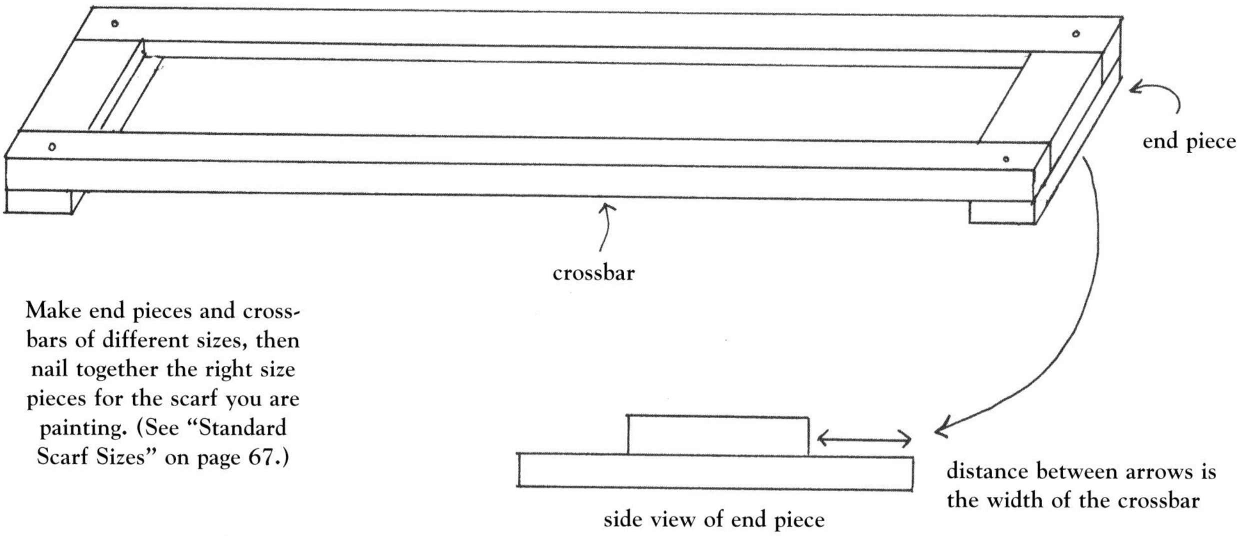

Make end pieces and crossbars of different sizes, then nail together the right size pieces for the scarf you are painting. (See "Standard Scarf Sizes" on page 67.)

Figure 6.4

you can see from Figure 6.4, it's very simple in design.

Attach the silk to the frame with stainless steel pins (available from silk-painting suppliers); common tacks will rust.

FINISHING SCARVES

If you purchase yardage, you can make the scarves any size you desire. Consider creating three long rectangular scarves at one time. Pin a 2-yard length of silk onto your frame. Use a resist to mark two lines an equal distance apart down the length of the silk to make three separate panels. Once the resist is thoroughly dry, you can color each of the three panels independent of one another. (This would be a great way to try all three silk-painting techniques described in Chapter 7.) When each painted panel is thoroughly dry, cut the panels apart to hem them.

HAND FINISHING

Run a length of silk thread through beeswax. Thread onto a #8 sewing needle; knot the end of the thread. Take the edge of the silk and roll it twice. Insert the needle and work a catch stitch around the edge of the scarf, as shown in Figure 6.5; tie off. This technique takes a bit of practice to do well; you may want to try the machine method instead.

MACHINE FINISHING

Place the hemmer foot on your machine. (See Fig. 6.6.) Turn the edge of the silk under 1/8 inch twice. Insert the silk under the presser foot and sew four stitches to secure it in place. (See Fig. 6.7.) Insert the needle into the fabric, then pull the folded cloth into the curved

Figure 6.5

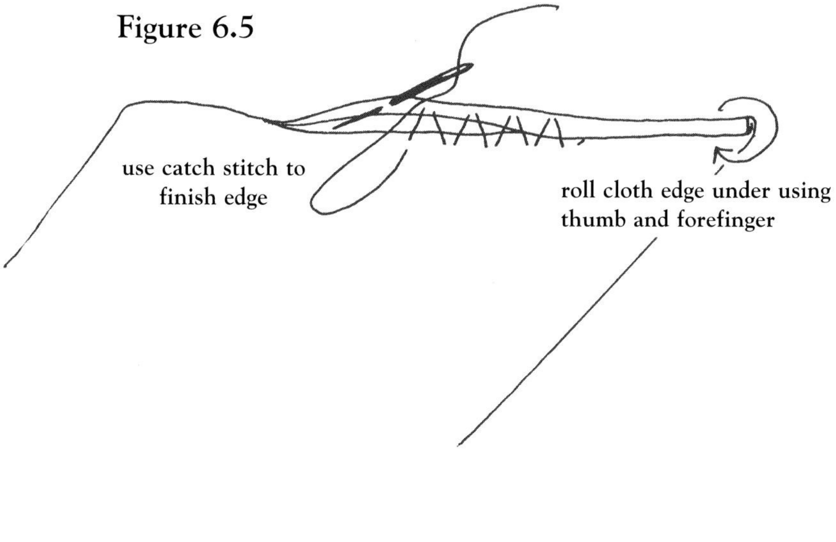

PAINTBRUSHES

Although I have recommended specific brushes for some projects, feel free to experiment and use whatever brush works best for you. Just be sure to use a quality brush for best results. This illustration, courtesy of Loew-Cornell, Inc., shows the wide variety of brush sizes and shapes available.

Care of Brushes. Brushes will last a long time if you cleam them thoroughly after each use. Be sure to clean the paint out of the hairs/fibers all of the way to the ferrule (the metal section that holds the brush together). Then stand the dry brushes, handle down, in a container. Or lay them flat and roll them in a carrying case.

Round - Use on point, or apply pressure to make thick-to-thin strokes.

Spotter - For fine detailing.

Liner - Continuous curved or straight lines. Vary thickness with pressure changes.

Ultra Round - Use as a liner on point. Full belly provides a reservoir for paint.

Jackie's Liner - Mid-length liner.

Script Liner (Long Liner) - Scroll work, flowing thick-to-thin lines. Length of hair holds more paint than a regular liner.

Shader (Flat) - Blocking in color, shading, blending, highlighting, and stroke work.

Chisel Blender (Bright) - Short, flat strokes and blénding, especially useful with heavy mediums.

Angular Shader (Angle Flat) - Tight shading, curved strokes. Popular rose petal brush.

Wash (Wash/Glaze) - Washes, basecoating and applying finishes.

One Stroke (Stroke) - Long, flat lettering brush.

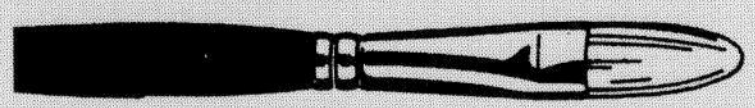

Filbert (Oval) - Strokes with soft edges. Blending. A natural flower petal shape.

Deerfoot Stippler - Texturizing brush. Use a dry brush and light, pouncing technique for fur, shrubbery, and soft backgrounds.

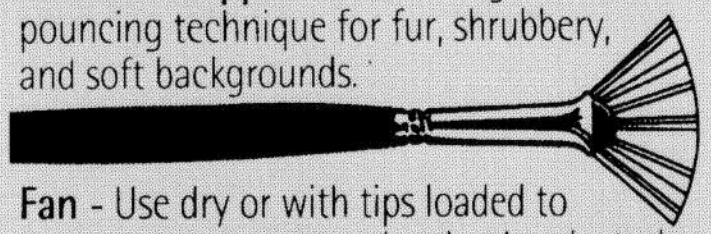

Fan - Use dry or with tips loaded to create texture or smooth other brush strokes.

Rake® - Flat, texturizing brush with a naturally-fingered shape. Use for hair, grass, wood grain, feathers, and fur. **Filbert Rake®** creates the same effect with softer edges.

Dagger Striper - Long chisel edge for easy, fine lines. Vary pressure for thick-to-thin ribbon effect.

Miracle-Wedge® - Can be easily loaded with 3 different colors for a variety of stroke effects.

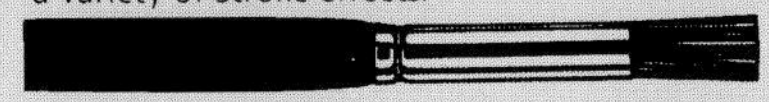

***Stencil** - Use a dry brush with very little paint and circular or stippling technique.

***Mop** - Blending and softening. Washes.

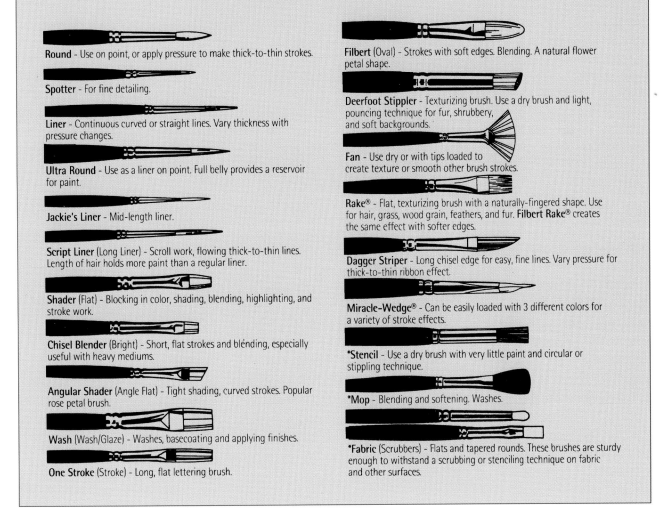

***Fabric** (Scrubbers) - Flats and tapered rounds. These brushes are sturdy enough to withstand a scrubbing or stenciling technique on fabric and other surfaces.

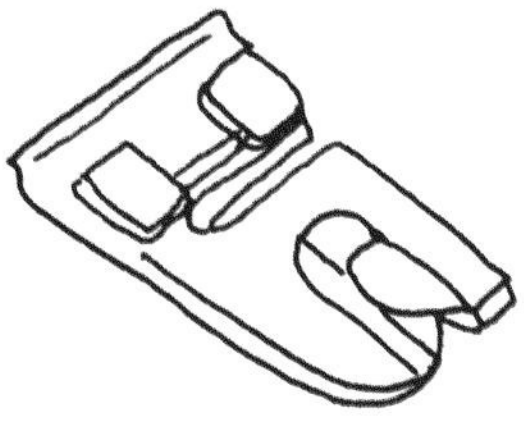

hemmer foot

Figure 6.6

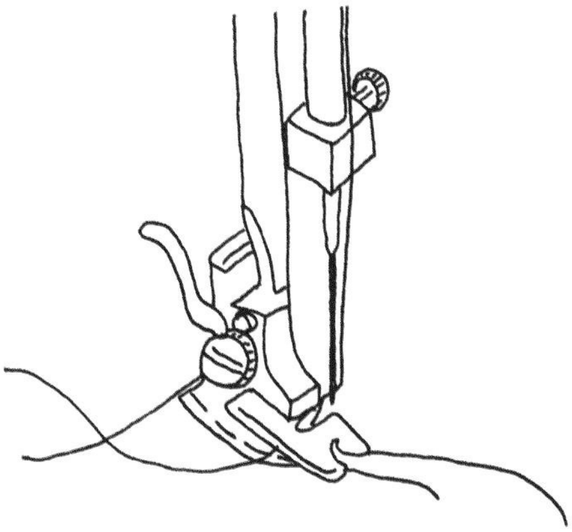

Figure 6.7

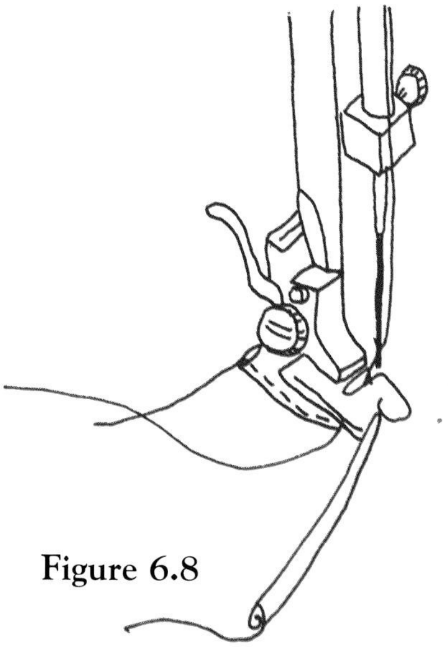

Figure 6.8

scroll section at the front of the hemmer foot. Make sure the threads are pulled to the back. Lower the presser foot, then begin sewing, continually holding the silk slightly up and to the left so that it feeds correctly onto the hemmer foot. (See Fig. 6.8.)

Leather

Soft, luscious leather is nice to the touch and extremely durable.

Cabretta leather, used for the bags shown in Chapter 7, is made from sheepskin and is very soft and luxurious. It's lightweight, too, so it won't be a bother on long shopping days. To construct these bags, you can also use deerskin, doe kidskin, or extra-soft cowhide. Suede, which has a napped texture, is a less expensive choice.

Leather and suede skins are priced by the square foot. Chamois (lambskin), readily available at most auto care centers, would work as well. Chamois is also sold as a skin.

Special diamond-shaped leather sewing machine needles are available for leatherwork. However, I have found an ordinary sewing needle (size 16) works just fine on thin, buttery leathers as long as it is sharp. Use what works best for you.

For leatherwork, set your machine for a straight stitch with approximately ten stitches per inch. Do not pin the leather pieces together for sewing; pins will leave permanent holes. Instead, use rubber cement, if necessary. You can also use rubber cement to permanently bond raw edges for a nice clean finish.

The beauty of leather is that it is so easy to care for. If it gets dusty, wipe it off with a dry cloth. If it gets soiled from use, just use a slightly damp cloth to bring back the luster. Over the years, leather will age and develop a beautiful patina.

CHAPTER 7

THE ESSENTIAL ACCESSORIES

Silk Scarves, Hats, Bags & Belts

Take a ho-hum outfit and make it smashing by adding the essential accessories. Dangle a silk scarf over the shoulder of your power suit, or use the scarf as a hip wrap over a party dress. Hats, bags, and belts add the finishing touch to creative dressing.

FLUID FLOURISHES: HAND-PAINTED SILK SCARVES

Hand-paint your own beautiful scarves. Shown here are Chasing Butterflies (left), Monet's Rose Garden (center), Synchronized Loops (right).

In the following projects, we'll explore three different techniques used for painting on silk. Each is unique in the way it is accomplished and in the final effect.

The first, and easiest, is a watercolor technique that results in a very soft-edged design with an ethereal, impressionistic feeling (like the one in the center scarf on page 74, Monet's Rose Garden).

The second technique creates actual representational shapes using resists (Chasing Butterflies, on the left). The third, a more advanced technique, combines watercolor with an applied design. This last project, Synchronized Loops (at right), also makes use of salt to achieve special effects.

The painted scarves in these projects are fixed with a chemical fixative. As one supplier told me, "Americans are resistant to steam setting." So I have used the alternative method here. The only difference between chemical wash and steam set is the intensity of color: The steam method produces a sharper color saturation. Either method produces excellent results. (For a detailed description of steam setting, see the two books on silk painting in Recommended Reading.)

MONET'S ROSE GARDEN

MATERIALS

- Rectangular silk scarf, prehemmed or yardage
- Jacquard or Deka silk paint/dye—yellow, cerise, green, and gray
- Chemical fixative

TOOLS & SUPPLIES

- Cloth scissors, if using yardage
- Adjustable fabric frame
- Stainless steel silk tacks
- Plastic wrap
- Paint containers
- Distilled water (if your tap water is hard)
- Spray bottle
- #12 round paintbrush
- Water jar (for rinsing paintbrush)
- Iron
- Ironing board
- Sewing machine or needle and thread

PROCEDURE

1. Cut a piece of silk for the scarf, or use a prehemmed scarf. Pin the silk in place on the fabric frame using the stainless steel tacks; place the tacks about 1 inch apart. Pull the silk taut, yet not so tight that holes appear near the tacks. Cover the work area with plastic wrap. Pour the paint into the containers.

2. To create the watercolor effect, you need to moisten the fabric so the paint can flow freely. In watercolor painting, this is called working "wet-in-wet." Using the spray bottle,

spray the silk with water until the fabric is moistened, but not dripping wet. Keep the bottle handy to remoisten areas as you work.

3. Look at the diagram of the silk scarf design (Fig. 7.0) to get a general idea of how the colors are applied. The unique quality of the watercolor technique is the creation of free-flowing, softly edged shapes. No two scarves done in this technique will be exactly the same.

4. Load your brush with yellow paint. Dot the brush where the flower centers will be located. Rinse the brush, then load it with cerise paint. Touch the fabric a few inches away from the yellow areas. Notice how the paint automatically spreads right up to the yellow. It may even mix a bit with it and create a small area of orange. If the paint is placed too close to a precolored area, it will envelop it and change it to a new color. In this instance, the yellow center would turn pure orange. Use this wicking effect to blend beautiful backgrounds. However, in this design, paint in the green first to subtly suggest foliage, then use the gray for the background.

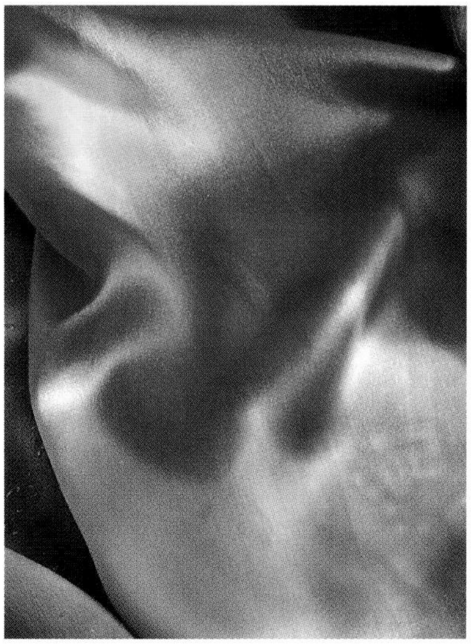

Not only did Claude Monet, the noted impressionist, paint exquisite paintings, he was also an avid gardener. This scarf suggests the rose garden on a misty morning in Giverny, France.

5. Allow the painted scarf to dry on the frame for 24 hours. Prepare the chemical fixative, and fix according to the directions on the bottle. Hang the scarf to dry, then iron on a cool setting.

6. If you have used silk yardage, finish the scarf edges by hand or machine.

NOTE: The scarf shown on the cover was created using the rainbow watercolor technique—a variation of the above technique in which the dye colors are allowed to flow more freely. The moistened undecorated scarf is laid on a sheet of plastic wrap (no frame is needed), and the dye colors are simply dabbed on the scarf in a random pattern. I used all of the primary colors (red, yellow, blue) and secondary colors (orange, green, purple) in small batches along the length of the scarf. As the colors mingled, they created a rainbow effect.

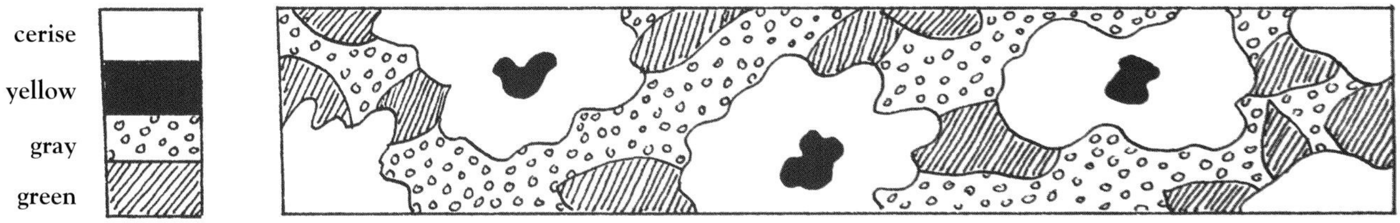

Figure 7.0

CHASING BUTTERFLIES

MATERIALS

Square silk scarf, prehemmed or yardage
Jacquard or Deka silk paint/dye—blue, purple, yellow, black, orange
Clear gutta resist
Table salt
Chemical fixative

TOOLS & SUPPLIES

Cloth scissors, if using yardage
Adjustable fabric frame
Stainless steel tacks
Plastic wrap
Paint containers
Tracing paper
Gutta applicator bottle with fine tip
#12 round paintbrush (for large areas)
#6 round paintbrush (for small areas)
Cotton swabs
Water jar (for rinsing paintbrushes)
Iron and ironing board
Sewing machine, or needle and thread

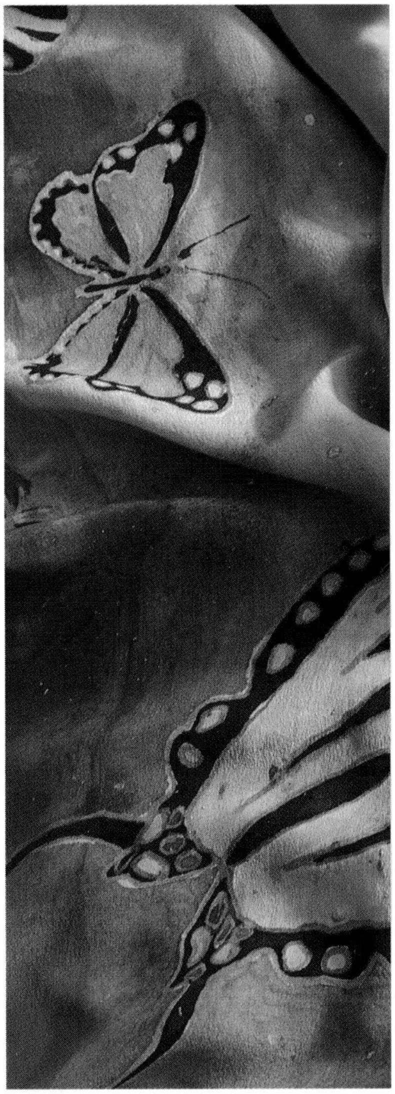

Capture butterflies to wear year-round! Swallowtails, monarchs, and the breezy little skippers flit about on this scarf. You'll be using the gutta resist technique, which is considered medium-difficult.

PROCEDURE

1. Cut a piece of silk for the scarf, or use a prehemmed scarf. Attach the silk to the fabric frame using the stainless steel tacks; place the tacks about 1 inch apart. Pull the silk taut, but not so tight that holes appear where the fabric is tacked. Cover the work surface with plastic wrap. Pour the paint into the containers.

2. Pour the gutta resist into the applicator bottle; attach the fine tip. You'll be applying the gutta in a thin line to make enclosed shapes. (See Fig. 7.1.) That way, the dye will remain within the shape without spreading into other areas of the design. When you use the resist, be sure it permeates the silk fibers and that the

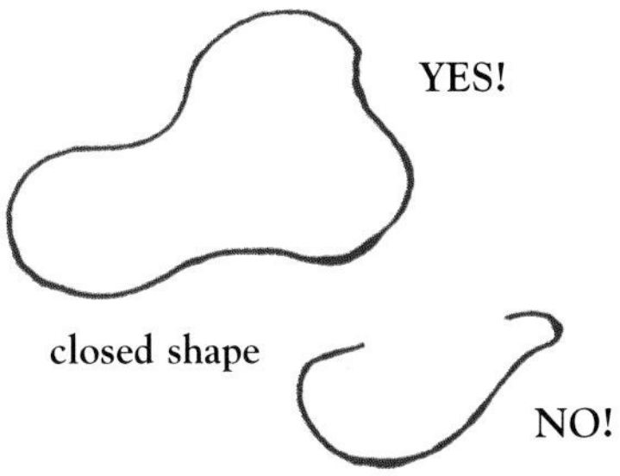

Figure 7.1

shapes outlined by the resist are unbroken.

3. See Figure 7.2 for the overall butterfly design. Using tracing paper, copy the individual butterfly designs shown in Figures 7.3 and 7.4. Trace the butterflies onto the silk by placing the traced butterflies under the scarf. You can trace the butterflies using the gutta, or you can trace them with a pencil, then go over the design with the gutta. Do it whichever way is more comfortable for you.

Let the resist dry thoroughly.

4. Using the color keys in Figures 7.3 and 7.4 as a guide, paint in the butterflies. (Use the smaller brush and the cotton swab to paint in the butterflies; use the larger paintbrush for large areas, such as the background. Be sure to rinse the brushes before applying a different color.) Paint in the background, beginning with the blue around the butterflies and working out to the purple border. Occasionally toss some salt onto the background to create a slight texturing and starburst effect. When you apply the purple, keep the area moist so the blue and purple will blend.

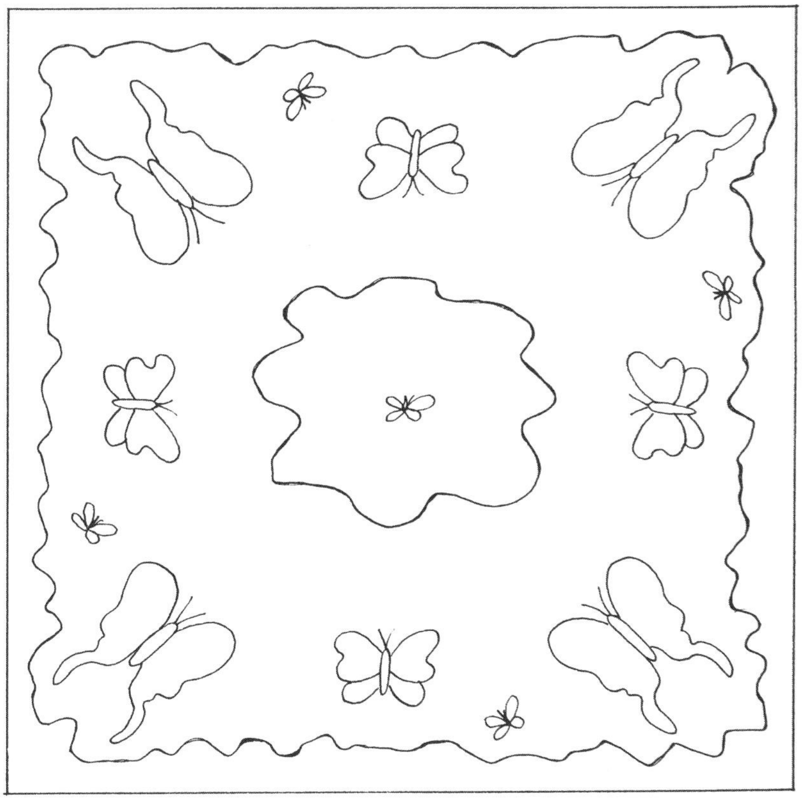

Figure 7.2

5. Allow the scarf to dry on the frame for 24 hours. Mix the chemical fixative, and fix the scarf according to the instructions on the bottle. Hang the scarf to dry, then iron on a cool setting.

6. If you have used silk yardage, finish the scarf edges by hand or machine.

Butterflies symbolize rebirth, free-spiritedness & beauty. A very exciting design motif!

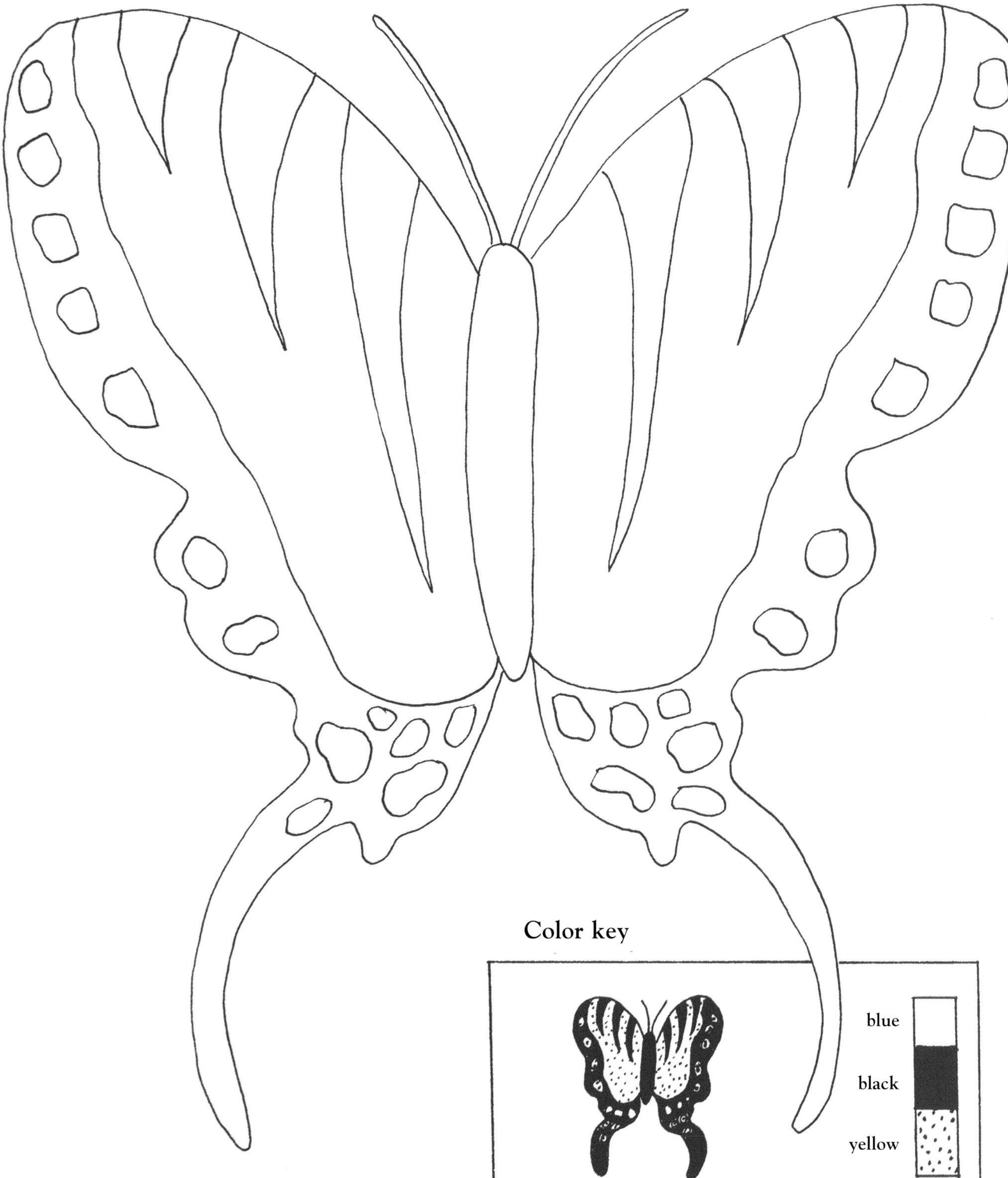

Figure 7.3

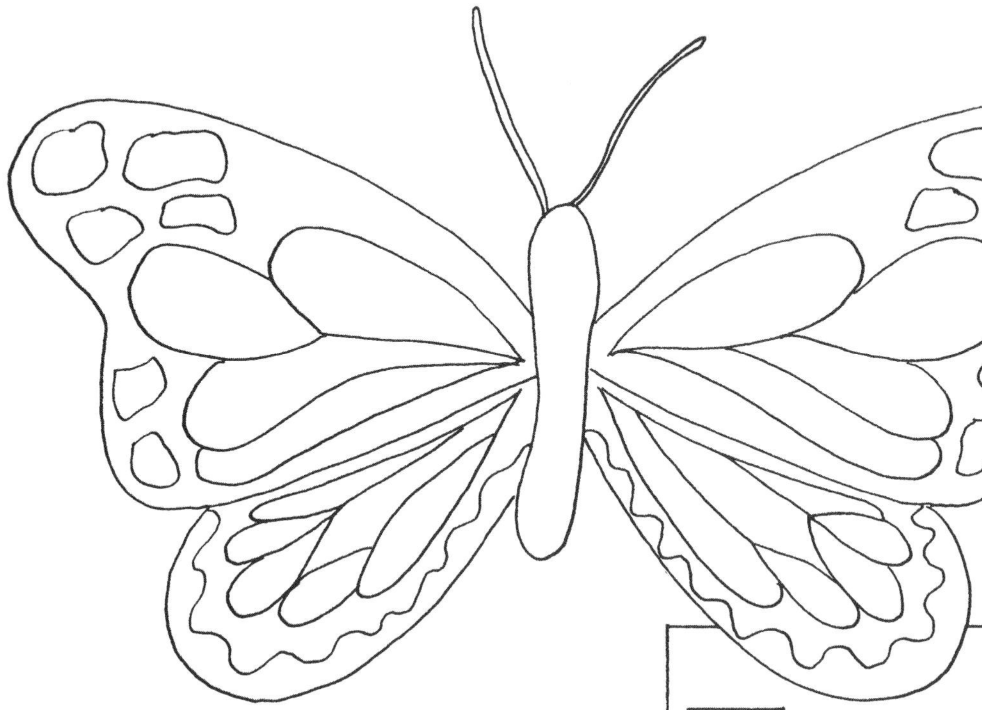

Color key

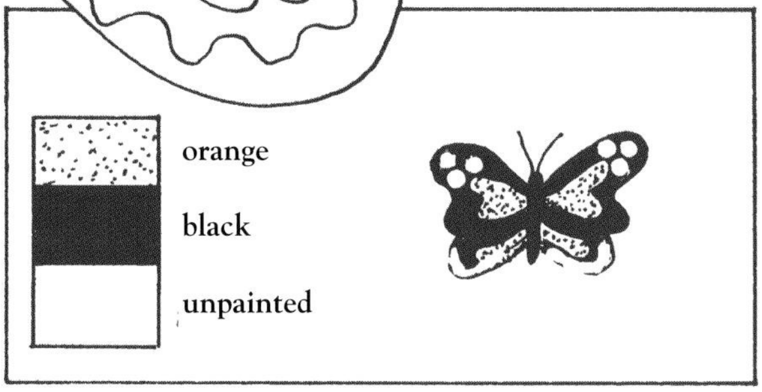

Figure 7.4

SYNCHRONIZED LOOPS

MATERIALS

Rectangular silk scarf, prehemmed or yardage
Jacquard or Deka silk paint/dye—blue, red
Table salt
Deka metallic gold silk paint
Chemical fixative

TOOLS & SUPPLIES

Cloth scissors, if using yardage
Adjustable fabric frame
Stainless steel tacks
Plastic wrap
Paint containers
Spray bottle
Distilled water—if your tap water is hard
#12 round paintbrush or foam pad
Paper towel
Fine-tip applicator bottle
Piece of white paper
Iron
Ironing board
Sewing machine, or needle and thread

The inspiration for this design came from raindrops falling into a puddle of water. You'll be using a watercolor technique to color the scarf in blues and purples, with accents created by salt applications. Decoration depicting swirling eddies is then applied with gold paint. Combining watercolor with the two other techniques makes this project advanced in its difficulty.

PROCEDURE

1. Cut the silk for the scarf, or use a prehemmed scarf. Attach the silk to the frame using stainless steel tacks placed about 1 inch apart. Cover the work surface with plastic wrap.

2. Mix up five different colors from the red and the blue paint: 1) For the first color, place some blue paint in a container and add water to create a dilution. 2) For the second color, place a capful of blue paint and a dash of water in a container. 3) For the third color, simply put pure blue paint in a container. 4) For the fourth color, put blue paint in a container and add a dash of red paint. 5) For the fifth color, place equal parts red and blue paint in a container.

3. Moisten the silk with water spray until the fabric is just moistened, not dripping wet. Using the paintbrush or paint pad, work the different colors—from light to dark—in a circular motion across the length of the silk. Squeeze the brush or pad with a paper towel to remove excess paint between color changes. Work fast; spray

Figure 7.5

with water as needed. While the paint is still wet, sprinkle on the salt; it will absorb some of the paint, creating even more color variation and a slightly textured look.

4. Allow the silk to dry on the frame, then place the fabric on the covered work surface. Place the gold paint in the applicator bottle; add the fine tip. Look at Figure 7.5 to get an idea of the kind of design you will be trying to achieve. Before applying the paint to the scarf, practice making concentric spirals on a piece of paper. Then look at the patterns of the blue/purple design on your scarf—you will see where to begin placing the spirals. Work the spirals across the length of the scarf. If you end up with an odd-shaped space between the spirals, use a solid shape. (See Fig. 7.5.) Allow the paint to dry thoroughly, then iron the scarf on the wrong side.

5. Mix the fixative, and fix the scarf according to the directions on the package.

6. If you have used yardage, finish the scarf edges by hand or machine.

According to Sara Bowman in *A Fashion for Extravagance*, during the 1910s painter and fashion designer Sonia Delauney became noted for her painted silks. She discovered a new way of using color when she executed a patchwork quilt for her new son, Charles. Delauney highlighted the element of movement in the fabric by using curvilinear shapes in her designs. Color and movement were an integral part of her theories on fabric design. The critics of the day stated that the silks were not mere fashion "but coherent compositions, living paintings, or sculpture, using living forms." The silks inspired Blaise Cendrars to pen the poem "On Her Dress She Wears A Body."

TOPPERS

HAND-DYED BASEBALL CAP

If you like hand-dyed cotton cloth done in gradations, this project is a good way to show off the beauty of the fabric. Each of the four cap panels, as well as the visor, uses a different piece of hand-dyed cloth ranging from intense to pale yellow. The center panel is made of a piece of multicolor dyed cloth appliquéd with flamboyant roses. You can find hand-dyed cotton at any quilting store. Keep in mind that depending on the fabric you choose for the front panel, you can change the color scheme of the cap to suit your tastes.

MATERIALS

- Gradated hand-dyed cotton, 6-tone range, each piece 8" × 10"
- 1 piece appliqué fabric of your choice, ½ yard
- 1 piece of multicolor dyed cotton, 8" × 10" (or use another piece of the yellow hand-dyed cotton), or piece of fabric of your choice
- Heavyweight iron-on interfacing
- Iron-on fusible webbing
- 3 roses cut from yardage, or other appliqués of your choice
- 1 piece of vinyl, 8" × 10"
- Yellow sewing thread
- Yellow grosgrain ribbon, 1 yard long, ⅜" wide

TOOLS & SUPPLIES

- Tracing paper
- Cloth scissors
- Iron
- Ironing board
- Sewing machine

PROCEDURE

1. Trace and cut out all the pattern pieces for this project, which you will find on pages 101 and 102. Then cut the pieces from the cotton you have selected. Fuse the interfacing to the back side of all cloth pieces to give the hat body.

2. Fold the top of the cap front (panel A), right sides together, so the "A"s match. (See Fig. 7.6.) Sew "A" and "A" together, using a ¼-inch seam allowance. Lock stitches at the beginning and end.

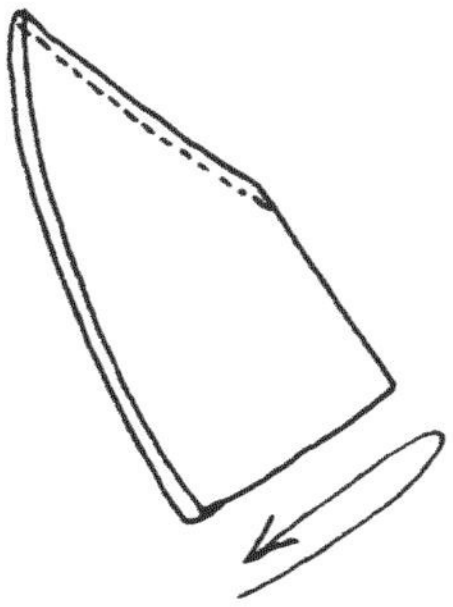

Figure 7.6

3. Decorate the cap front. Iron the fusible webbing onto the back of the appliqué yardage containing the motifs you wish to use on your cap. Cut out the motifs, then remove the paper backing. Iron the motifs in place on the cap front.

4. Place the first side piece (panel B) against the cap front, with right sides facing and the "A"s and "B"s matching. Sew from top to bottom, locking stitches. Sew the other side piece (panel B) to the other side of the cap front. (See Fig. 7.7.)

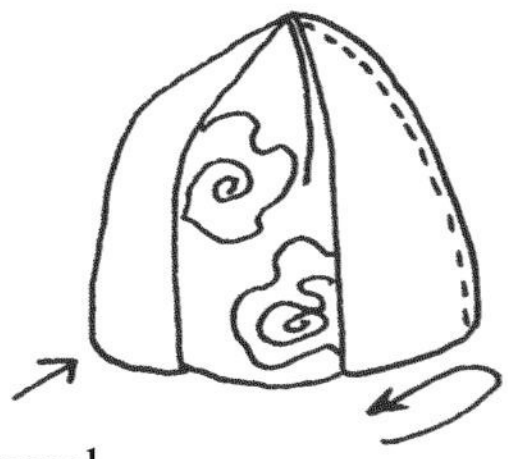

side panel

Figure 7.7

5. To finish the arched edge of each back (panel C), turn the arch under ⅛ inch, then another ⅛ inch, and edgestitch to hold. Repeat for the other cap back. (These pieces are mirror images, so be sure you are sewing the arch to the wrong side of the cloth!)

6. With right sides facing, match "A" and "C" of the cap side and back (panels B and C). Sew the pieces together, locking stitches at the beginning and end. Repeat for the other side of the cap.

7. Using a ¼-inch seam allowance, sew together the visor, right sides facing, going from "R" to "S" to "T". Trim the seam, then turn the visor right side out. Insert the vinyl in between the cloth. Pin to hold it tightly on the unsewn edge. Topstitch ¼ inch in from the front cap edge. Sew the inner arch ½ inch from the edge, removing pins as you sew. (See Fig. 7.8.) Trim this edge to ¼ inch.

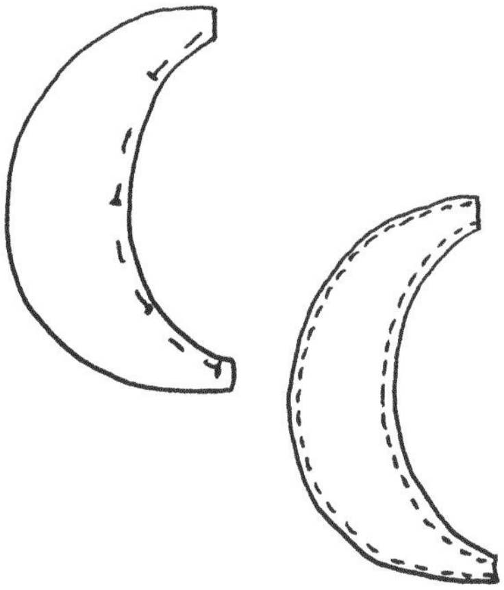

Figure 7.8

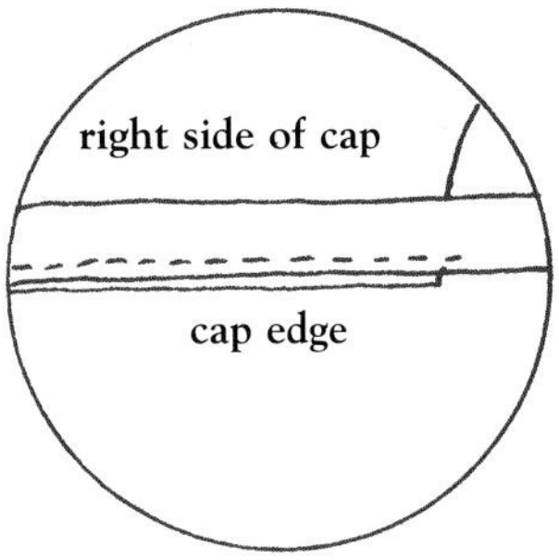

Figure 7.9

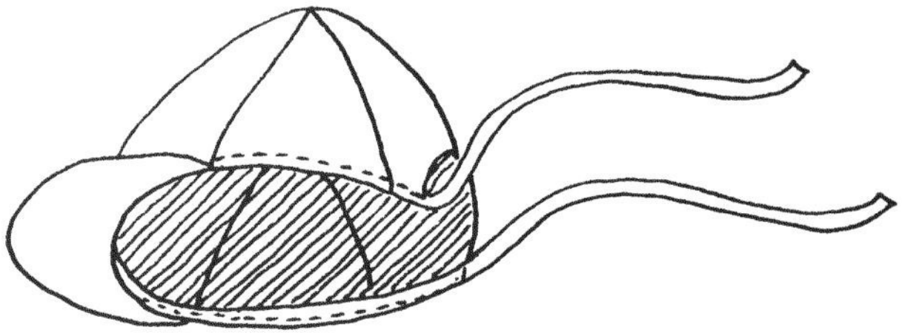

Figure 7.10

8. Match the center of the cap front with the center of the visor. Sew them together using a ¼-inch seam allowance.

9. Center the grosgrain ribbon on the inside of the cap front. Edgestitch the ribbon starting at the center of the cap front and continuing to the back. Lockstitch the end. (See Fig. 7.9.) Repeat for the other side. Turn the ribbon up, then from the outside of the cap, topstitch the ribbon in place as shown in Figure 7.10, working a triangle at the beginning and end of the stitching to reinforce the stress points at the back. (See Fig. 7.11.)

10. Try on the hat, then tie the ribbons to fit.

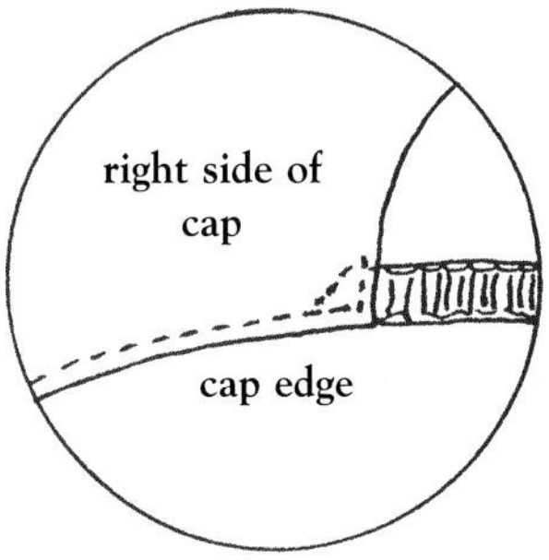

Figure 7.11

Blue Leaf Hat
by Roberta Z. Marco

This hat is made of satin, muslin, and Ultrasuede using painting, beading, and appliqué.

FLAME RED BOATER

Make your own fashion hat! This particular hat, called a boater because of its similarity to the hats worn by the Venetian gondoliers, sits on the back of the head. Done up in bright scarlet red, it is finished with millinery veiling and a wired adornment. You can use this basic hat technique to work up a bevy of hats out of different materials and with distinct adornments to suit your own whimsical style.

MATERIALS

- Red wool felt, 1 yard
- Red sewing thread (to match felt)
- Red grosgrain ribbon (to match felt), ¾" wide, 22" long
- Navy blue veiling shot with gold lamé threads, 9" × 35"
- Wired gold ribbon, 1½" wide, ⅝ yard

TOOLS & SUPPLIES

- Tracing paper
- Scissors
- Cloth scissors
- Sewing machine (with optional quilting attachment)
- #8 sewing needle
- Pins

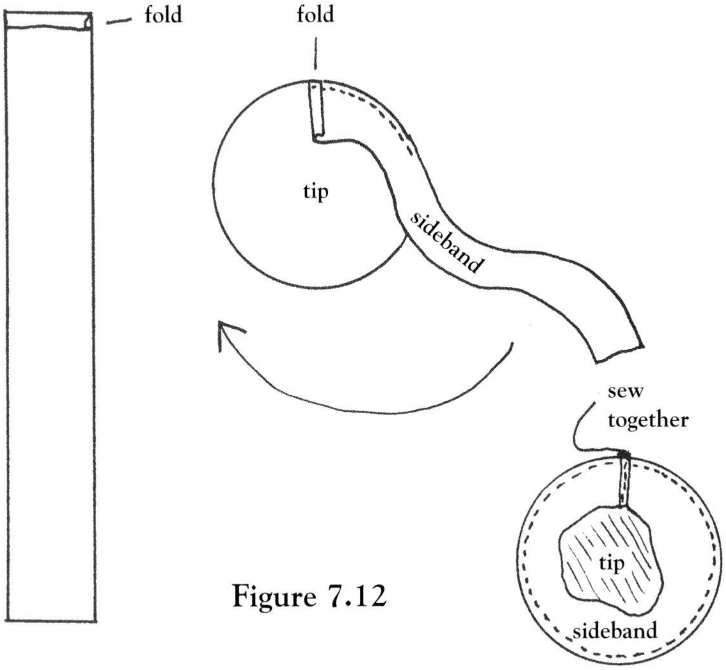

Figure 7.12

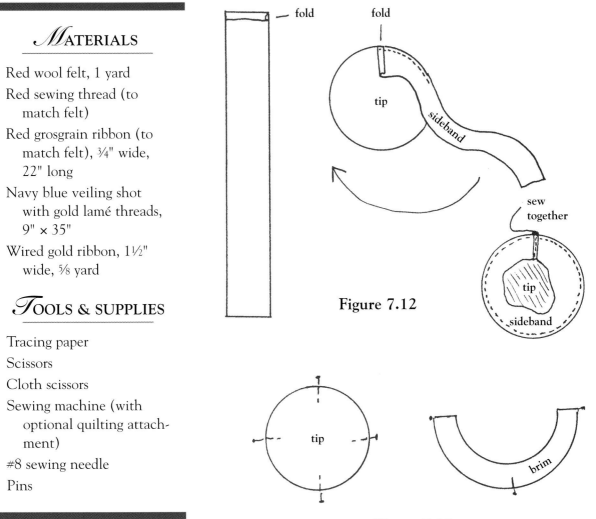

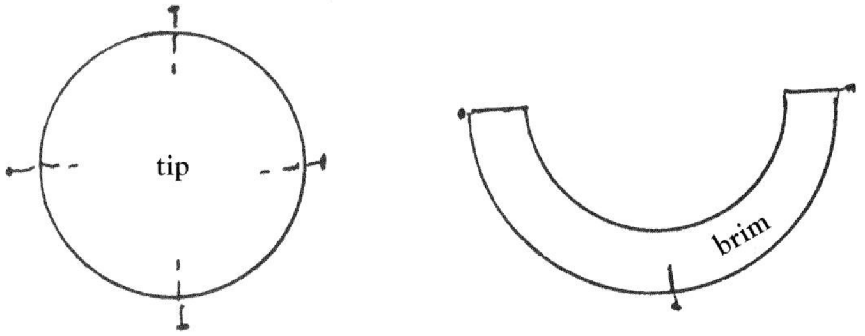

Figure 7.13

PROCEDURE

1. Trace and cut out all the pattern pieces for this project, which you will find on pages 103 and 104. Then cut the hat pieces from the felt.

2. Set the sewing machine to straight stitch. Fold one short side of the sideband up ¼ inch, and place it on the edge of the tip. Using a ½-inch seam allowance, sew the sideband to the tip of the hat. (See Fig. 7.12.) Backstitch at the end of the stitching. Remove the piece from the machine. Hold the ends of the sideband in a straight line and edgestitch toward the tip of the hat, as shown in Figure 7.12; backstitch. Do not trim away the seam allowance; this extra cloth helps shape the hat. (If you have a serger, you may wish to clean finish this edge.)

3. To locate the center of the sideband and the brim, fold each in half and insert pins to use as a guide when you sew the sideband to the brim. (See Fig. 7.13.) Ease as necessary to fit. Place the brim to the sideband and sew the pieces together using a ½-inch seam allowance. (See Fig. 7.14.) Backstitch the end; don't trim the seam.

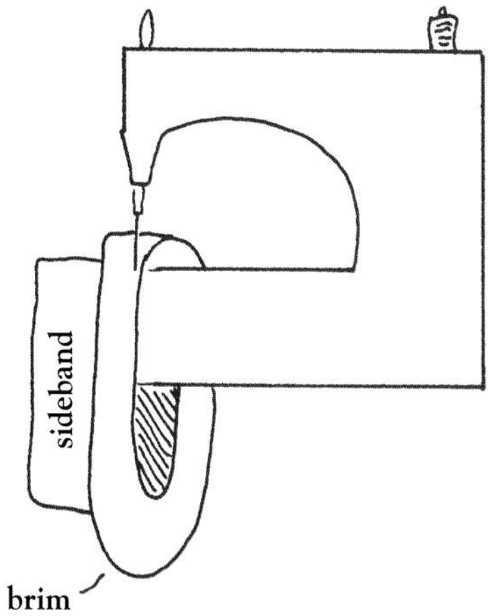

Figure 7.14

4. Place the hat on top of the second brim, and pin to hold the pieces together. Topstitch the brims together, working from the top of the hat edge where the brim is joined, to the sideband. (You may wish to use the quilting sewing machine attachment as a guide.) I spaced the stitching lines 7⁄16 of an inch apart—you can use more or fewer lines of topstitching. Just remember: The more lines of stitching, the firmer the brim. Backstitch at the beginning and end of the line of topstitching. Trim the outside edge of the brim close to the last line of stitching.

5. Lay the red grosgrain ribbon on the edge of the second brim seam allowance, beginning at the center back of your hat. Hand-sew the ribbon in place from the bottom of the hat. Stop sewing when you are within 1½ inches of the beginning. (See Fig. 7.15.) Turn the end of the ribbon under ½ inch, and sew the ribbon to the end. Turn the ribbon to the inside of the hatband, and whipstitch it in place.

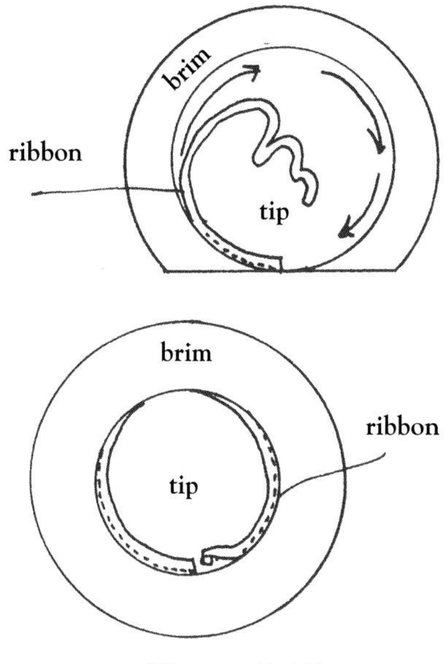

Figure 7.15

6. Wind the veiling around the sideband of the hat. Tack it in place at the back of the hat so that the ends hang free. (See Fig. 7.16.) Wind the wired ribbon into 1-inch loops as shown in Figure 7.17, then sew the ribbon adornment in place at the back of the hat.

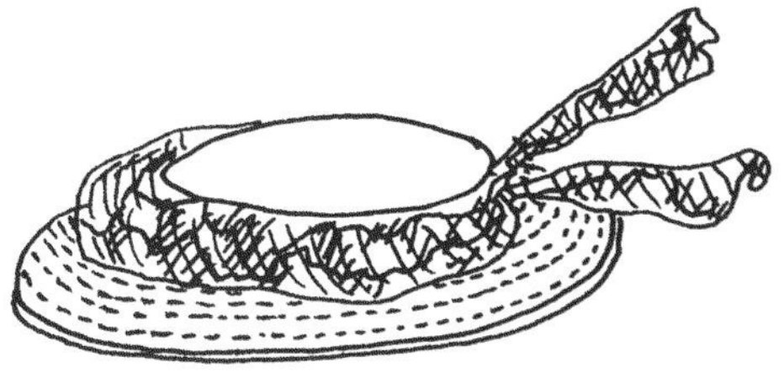

Figure 7.16

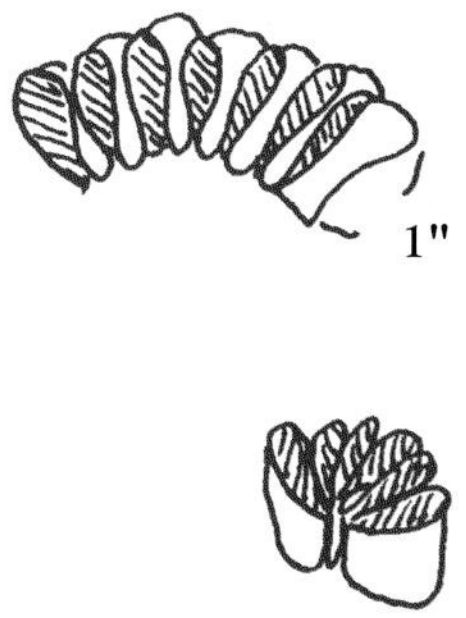

Figure 7.17

STASH IT!

Even undecorated, leather makes a posh statement. These bags show two unique ways to accentuate your style by starting with this naturally supple material. Leather can be expensive, so watch for sales or look for leather garments at resale shops. If leather is not within your budget, try using suede instead.

THISTLE CUTWORK BAG

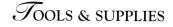

Enhance the natural elegance of leather by adding sophisticated cutwork. With just a few snips, you can create a smashing design. You'll love carrying this clever drawstring bag.

MATERIALS

- 1 skin soft leather
- 1 piece of leather or suede, 7½" × 9", for the inset
- 8 gold metal seed beads, size 11
- Thread (to match the leather)

TOOLS & SUPPLIES

- Utility knife
- Tracing paper
- Scissors
- Sewing machine
- Leather sewing machine needle
- Rubber cement
- Rubber cement remover
- Utility paintbrush
- #8 sewing needle
- White glue
- Cardboard (optional)

PROCEDURE

1. Cut two pieces of leather measuring 8¾ inches by 12½ inches for the bag front and back. Trace the pattern for the bag bottom on page 105, and use it to cut out an oval of leather.

2. To make the bag cord, cut a piece of leather 1 inch wide and 45 inches long; piece the leather together if necessary. Fold the strip in half lengthwise, matching the edges carefully. Edgestitch as shown in Figure 7.18, then set the piece aside.

3. Trace the thistle design pattern on page 105 and transfer it to the center of the bag front. Carefully cut out the design using a utility knife. (It is easier to cut out the smallest areas first, then the larger areas.) Lay the inset piece under the cutwork area, then trace the cutwork design onto the inset. Apply the rubber cement to the inset, avoiding the thistle design. Use a paintbrush to apply the rubber cement close to the thistle design; let it dry. Apply the rubber cement to the back of the leather piece with the cutout thistle design; let it dry. Remove the rubber cement from the brush with the cement remover. Carefully place the inset and the leather cutout piece together.

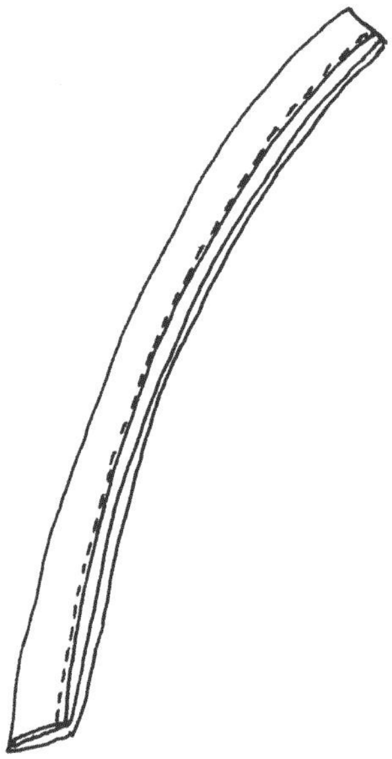

Figure 7.18

4. Sew the beads in place at the center of the thistle.

5. Using a ½-inch seam allowance, sew the bag front and back together, with right sides facing. Using a ¼-inch seam allowance, place right sides together, and sew the oval in place at the bottom of the bag. (Check the cutwork design to be sure you are sewing the bottom oval to the correct side of the bag!) Turn the bag right side out.

6. To make the top casing, turn down the top edge 1½ inches to the inside of the bag. Sew 1 inch from the top edge. Snip the threads on one of the side seams to leave an opening for the casing. Dot the thread ends with white glue; let dry. Insert the leather cord in the casing. Bring the ends of the leather cord together, and tie them in an overhand knot. Trim the strap ends, if necessary. Dot the thread ends with white glue.

7. If you prefer a stiffer bottom for your bag, use the bottom pattern (minus ¼ inch all around) to cut out a piece of cardboard. You can cover the cardboard with a piece of leather for a nice finish.

FLAP BAG WITH SHELL MEDALLION

Here, a classic pouch-style bag with a simple gold chain is embellished with a large medallion ornate with shells, embroidery, and beads. This fine bag can go anywhere with anything. The medallion on this piece has Spanish and Native American design influences. It can also be interpreted as a mandala—the Hindu or Buddhist symbol of the universe.

PROCEDURE

FOR BAG:

1. Cut a piece of leather 9 inches by 9 inches for the bag front. Cut a 9-by-13½-inch leather piece for the bag back.

2. Place the two leather pieces together, right sides facing, so the shorter piece is flush to one end of the longer leather piece. Using a ½-inch seam allowance, sew the sides together, then sew across the bottom. (See Fig. 7.19.) Reinforce the top edge of the seam by taking a few discreet hand stitches.

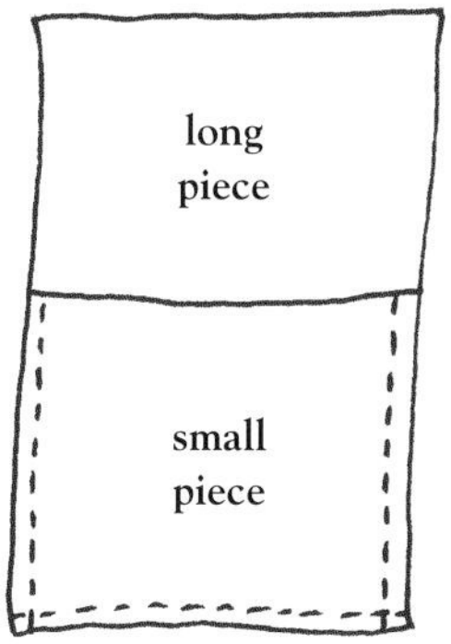

Figure 7.19

MATERIALS

FOR BAG:

1 skin soft leather
Thread (to match leather)
Gold chain, 42"
3 jump rings, 12mm

FOR MEDALLION:

Black wool felt, 4" × 8"
White wool felt, 2" square
Embroidery floss—white, chestnut brown, black
1 shark eye shell, or any other interesting flat-topped shell about 1½" in diameter
19 whelk shell slices, or other shells that can be strung
19 gold seed beads, size 8

TOOLS & SUPPLIES

Utility knife
Sewing machine
Leather sewing machine needle
#10 sewing needle
Ruler
Cloth scissors
Rubber cement
Jewelry pliers
#8 sewing needle

3. Fold the bag bottom so that the side seam and bottom seam are aligned. (See Fig. 7.20.) Measure and mark 1½ inches up from the seam point. Use a ruler to mark the stitching line across the bag corner. (See Fig. 7.21.) Machine-sew across the corner. Knot the thread ends close to the leather, then clip away the excess thread. Repeat for the other corner. Do not clip off the triangle flaps; glue them in place with the rubber cement to stabilize the bag bottom. Turn the bag right side out.

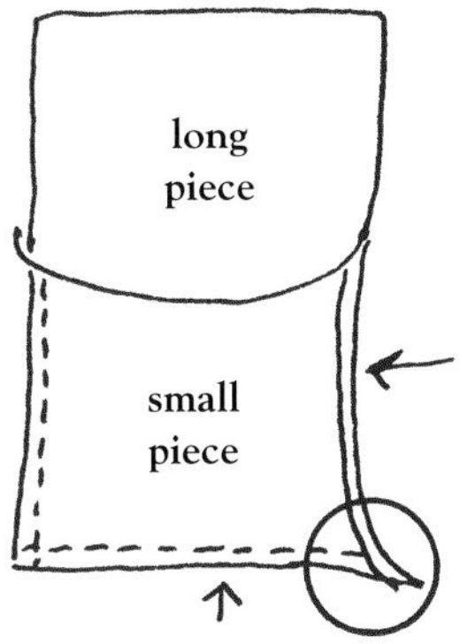

Figure 7.20

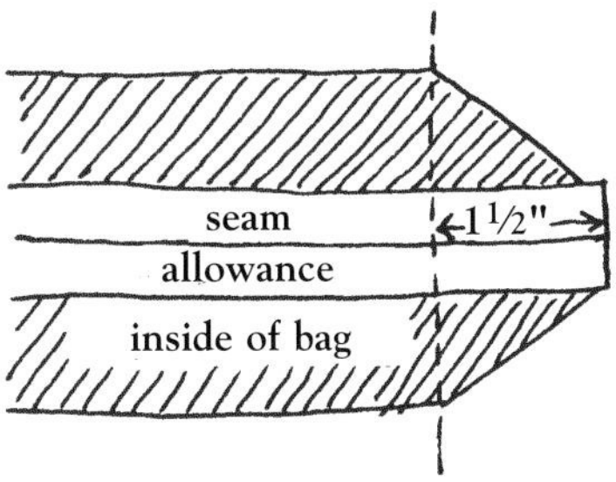

Figure 7.21

4. To finish off the bag flap, fold the sides to the inside ½ inch, then fold the top down ½ inch. (See Fig. 7.22.) Make crisp folds. Apply rubber cement inside the flaps—first the sides, then the top flap. Weight down the bag flap, and allow the rubber cement to set for at least a few hours.

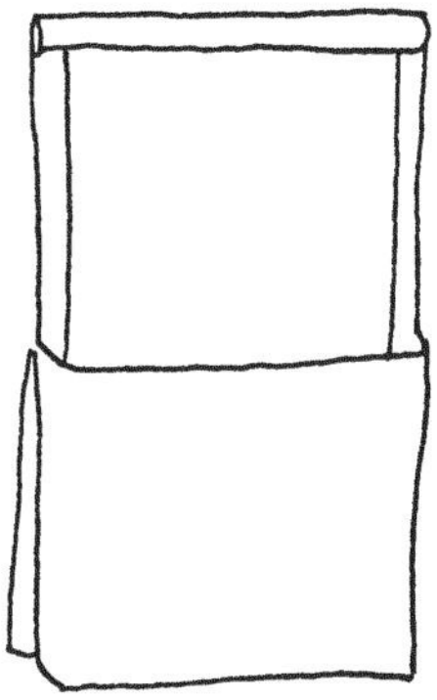
Figure 7.22

5. Attach the ends of the chain with a jump ring to form a continuous loop of chain. (See Chapter 1 for details on how to use jump rings.) Measure and mark 1¼ inches in from the outside edge of the inside bag flap. (See Fig. 7.23.) Using tiny stitches, sew a jump ring to each mark. (See Fig. 7.24.) Open the jump rings and attach the chain. Close the jump rings.

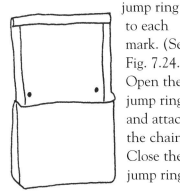

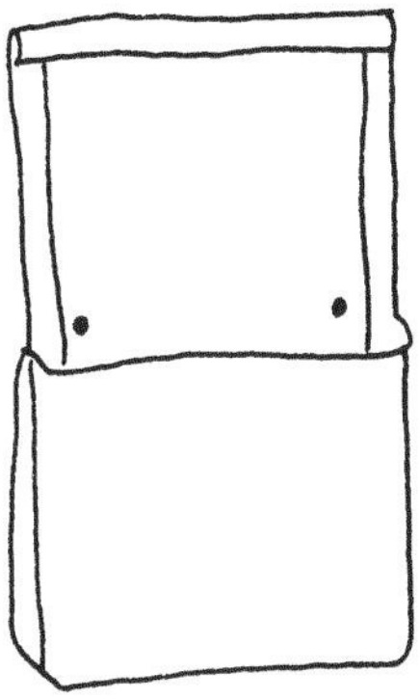
Figure 7.23

Figure 7.24

FOR MEDALLION:

6. Trace the pattern for the medallion on page 106, then cut two ovals from the black wool felt. Using Figure 7.25 as a guide, add the embroidery: With the ovals together, work blanket stitch, as shown in Figure 7.26, around the outside edge in white floss. Do a circle of chain stitches, as shown in Figure 7.27. Then work the diagonals, as shown in Figure 7.28. Switch to brown thread and work French knots, as shown in Figure 7.29, to alternate with the diagonals.

7. Use the shell collar pattern on page 106 to cut out the white felt shell collar. Adjust the inside cutout as necessary to fit the large shell you have chosen to use. Work the diagonal stitch in brown floss on the edge of the inside hole. (See Fig. 7.30.) Hold the shell on the center of the medallion, then place the felt collar over the shell and baste the edge of the collar in place. Embroider a line of chain stitches in brown floss over the basting stitches. Make a row of French knots in black floss on the collar edge. Sew on a row of gold beads to alternate with the French knots. Sew a row of chain stitches in brown floss next to the line of white chain stitches where the collar meets the black felt oval.

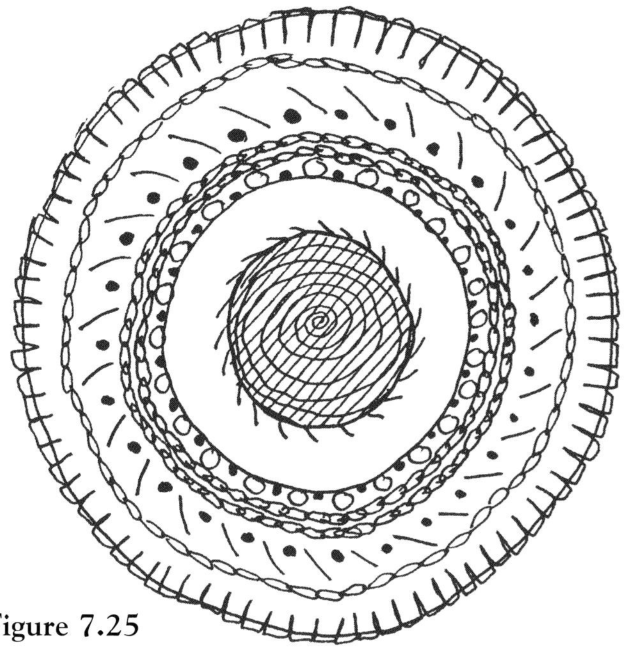

Figure 7.25

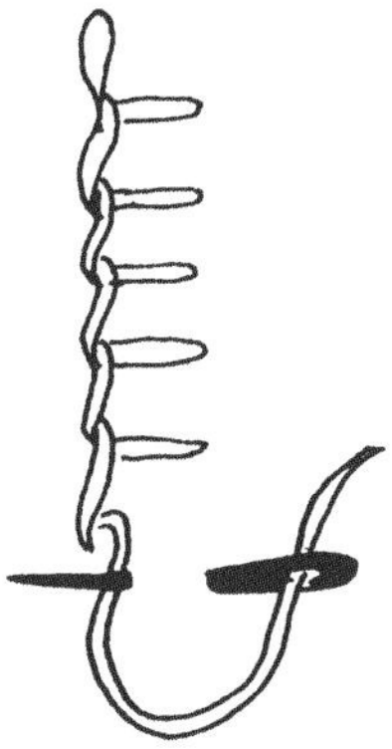

Figure 7.26

Figure 7.27

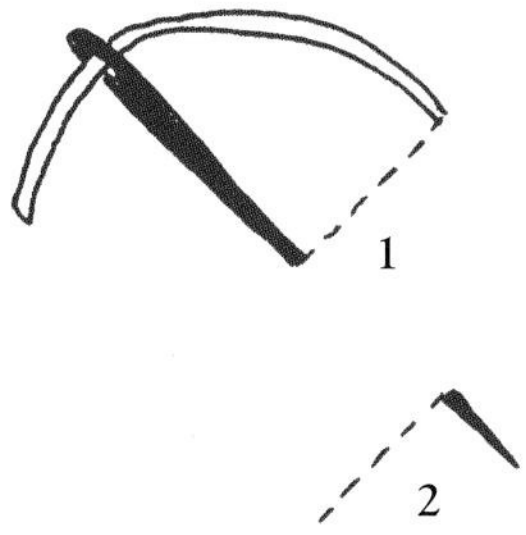

Figure 7.28

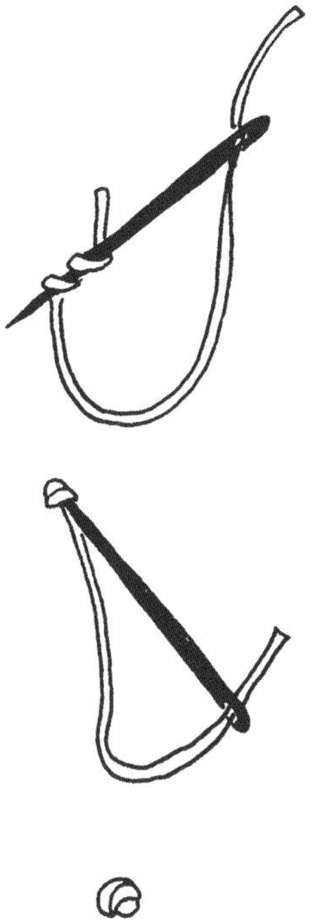

Figure 7.29

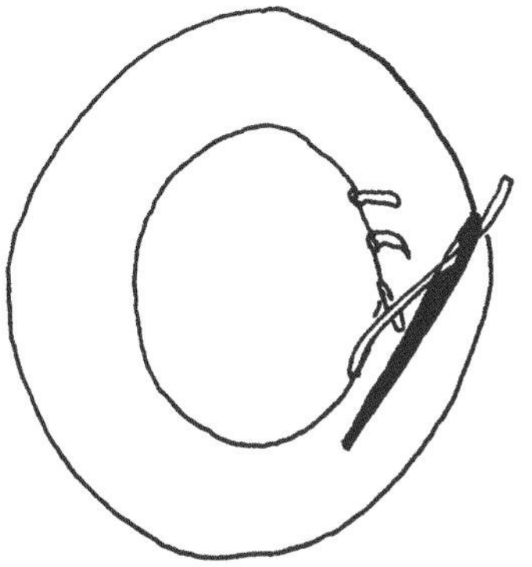

Figure 7.30

8. Using black floss, sew on the shell fringe. Insert the needle from the back of the medallion, add the shell, knot the thread around the shell, then insert the needle back into the medallion. Come up about ¼ inch from the first shell, and repeat until you have added all the shells. Tie off the thread on the back of the medallion. Clip away any excess thread. Sew the medallion in place on the bag flag using long stitches of floss. (See Fig. 7.31.)

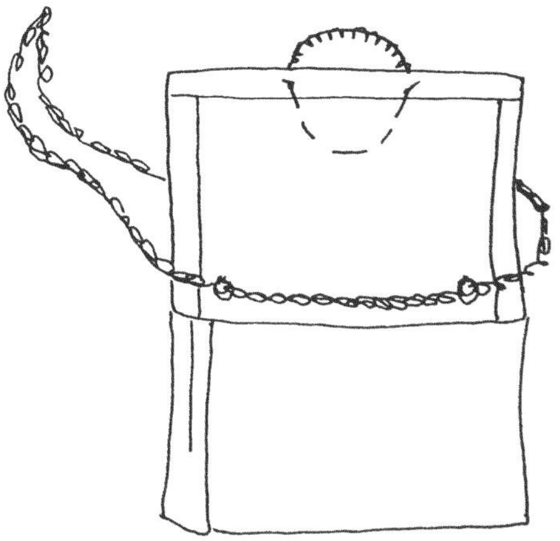

Figure 7.31

WAIST ACCENTS

PEACOCK FEATHER BELT

Show off the beauty of the natural colors in a single peacock feather—the intense blue, green, and metallic gold-bronze—in this stylish belt. Wear it on a simple black sheath for nighttime, or pair it up with denim for casual chic.

MATERIALS

Peacock feather (available at import stores)

Black cotton cloth, ½ yard, 45" wide

Clear vinyl, medium weight, 5" × 8" and 1½" × 40"

Black Ultraleather, ¼ yard

Black Velcro, 6¾"

Black sewing thread

Madeira gold thread

YLI Pearl Crown Rayon, navy blue

YLI Metallic, chartreuse green

Jacquard StarBright fabric paint, #418 black

Deka fabric paint—gold, silver

Cardboard, 3" square

TOOLS & SUPPLIES

Rotary cutter

#12 round paintbrush

Glue stick

Sewing machine

#8 sewing needle

PROCEDURE

1. Measure your waist and add 7 inches. This is measurement A.

2. Using the rotary cutter, cut two 1½-inch wide strips of black cotton 1½ times measurement A. Separate the cotton strips. Load the brush with paint, and let it drop onto the cloth. Use each of the different paints, as little or as much as you choose. Use the silver paint for discreet highlights. Let the paint dry thoroughly.

3. Using the Peacock Feather Belt Pattern on page 106, cut out the vinyl and two pieces of black cotton. To make the buckle, lay the feather on the black cotton. Cut off the excess feather shaft, then pick up the feather and dab the back with the glue stick. Place it back on the black cotton; lay the vinyl on top. Edgestitch around the entire piece.

4. From the Ultraleather, cut four ½-inch wide strips using the rotary cutter. Sew them into a strip. To add the binding to the peacock feather buckle, turn the buckle wrong side up. Lay an Ultraleather strip right side down, flush with the outer edge. (See Fig. 7.32a.) Using a straight stitch, sew ¼ inch from the edge around buckle. Turn the buckle right side up. Turn the binding to the front, and turn it under ¼ inch.

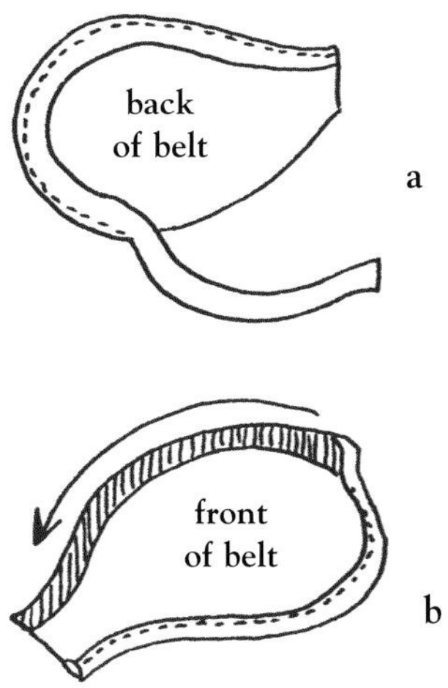

Figure 7.32

Edgestitch it in place. (See Fig. 7.32b.)

5. Cut a strip of vinyl the same size as the cloth strips; piece if necessary. Use the glue stick to glue the vinyl strip between the two black cotton strips, making sure the painted side of the cotton faces outward. Edgestitch the pieces together. Using the same method as you did for the buckle, sew the binding in place on either side of the long strips.

6. Finish one end of the belt by cutting a tab 1½ inches by 2 inches from the Ultraleather. Fingerpress the tab ¼ inch up on either side, then ¼ inch up on the two remaining sides. (See Fig. 7.33.) Place the longer folded edge on the end of the belt, wrong side down; edgestitch. Flip the tab to the other side of the belt. (The raw edge should be turned under ¼ inch.) Edgestitch. (See Fig. 7.34.)

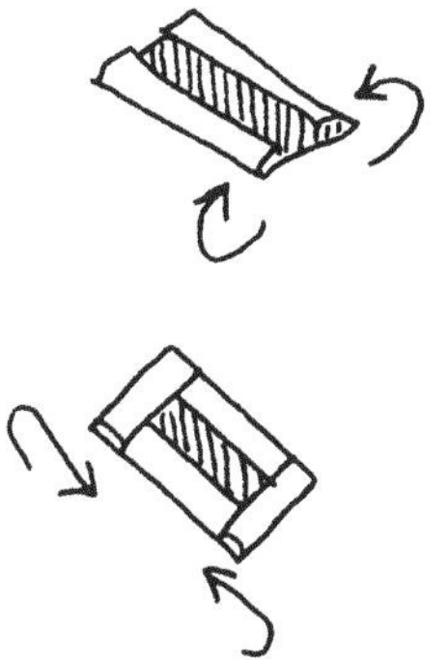

Figure 7.33

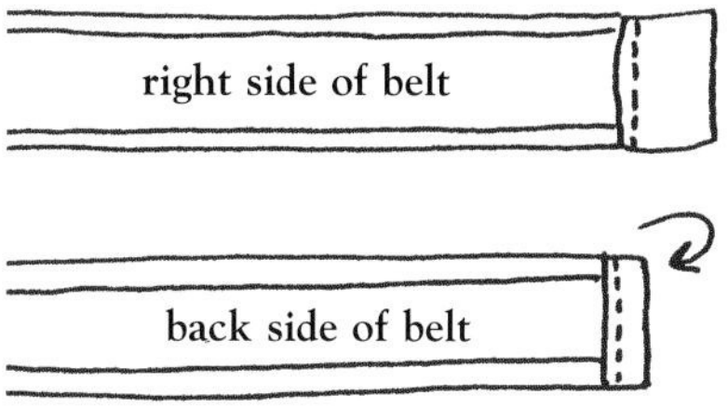

Figure 7.34

7. Attach the other end of the belt to the buckle; lay the buckle face down. Overlap the raw edge of the belt ½ inch over the small end of the buckle, then zigzag them together. (See Fig. 7.35.)

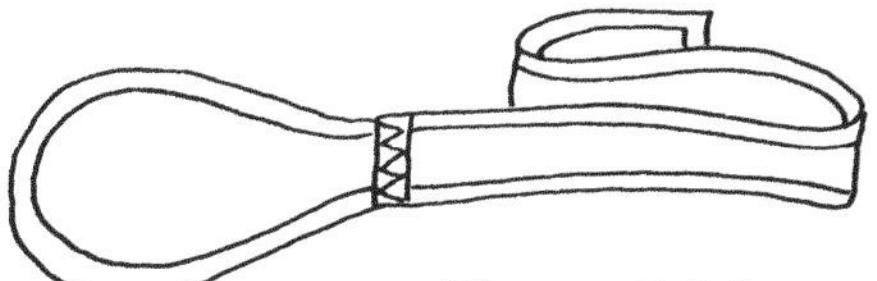

Figure 7.35

8. Cut two strips of black cotton 1¾ inches by 7½ inches. Stack the strips. Using a ¼-inch seam allowance, sew all around the strips, leaving one of the long ends open for turning. Clip the corners, then turn the piece right side out. Fingerpress the raw edge ¼ inch to the inside; edgestitch it closed. Edgestitch the looped side of the Velcro strip on the black cloth strip. Lay this strip onto the back of the buckle. (See Fig. 7.36.) Sew in place only on the short ends of the strip. Edgestitch the soft strip of Velcro to the other end of the belt. (To be sure that you are sewing the Velcro to the correct side of the belt, you can wrap the belt around your waist, then mark the side with a pin.)

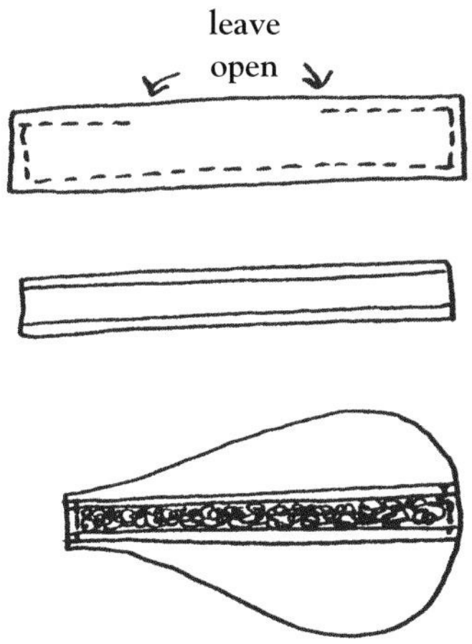

Figure 7.36

9. To make the tassel, wrap the chartreuse thread around the cardboard 12 times; wrap the navy blue thread around the cardboard 20 times. Take a 6-inch length of black thread, run it under the threads, and tie it in a knot. Snip the thread from the spools, and cut the threads at the bottom to remove the cardboard. (See Fig. 7.37.) Stroke all the threads down from the top. Tie on the gold metallic thread about ½ inch down from the top. Wrap it around 20 times, then tie it off. Trim away the excess thread. Using black thread, sew the tassel in place on the belt. Trim the ends of the tassel, and fluff.

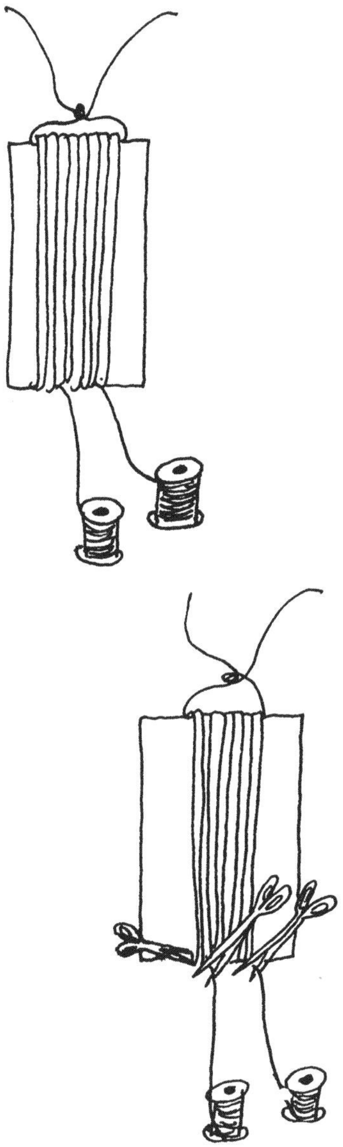

Figure 7.37

CONFETTI BELT

Bits of cloth, threads, and yarns create a wonderful one-of-a-kind belt. Make one up to match a favorite outfit, or take a look at your closet and create one in the predominant colors of your wardrobe.

PROCEDURE

1. Lay the strip of white cotton on the ironing board. Sprinkle on the "confetti," making a nice mix along the length of the cloth. Make sure the confetti doesn't stray beyond the edge of the cloth. Cut a strip of Heat-n-Bond to the size of the white cotton cloth, minus 1/4 inch all around. Lay the webbing on top of the confetti; fuse. (See Fig. 7.38.) Remove the paper backing. Lay the piece of nylon netting on top of the confetti. Cover with the backing sheet removed from the webbing. Press, then remove the paper.

2. Fold both long sides of the confetti cloth under 1/4 inch. (See Fig. 7.39.) Fingerpress both long sides of the leather belt under 1/4 inch. Apply rubber cement between the folds. Weight it down and allow to dry. Position the con-

MATERIALS

Soft gray leather, 2½ times your waist measurement plus 7"
Strip of white cotton cloth, same size as the belt
Fragments of cloth, ribbon, ribbon floss, threads, metallic threads, thin yarns—snipped into tiny pieces to make the "confetti"
Heat-n-Bond fusible webbing
White nylon netting, same size as the belt
Goldtone belt buckle
Gold metal beads, size 11
Gold metallic thread
Gray sewing thread (to match leather)

TOOLS & SUPPLIES

Cloth scissors
Ironing board
Iron
Sewing machine
Rubber cement
#8 sewing needle

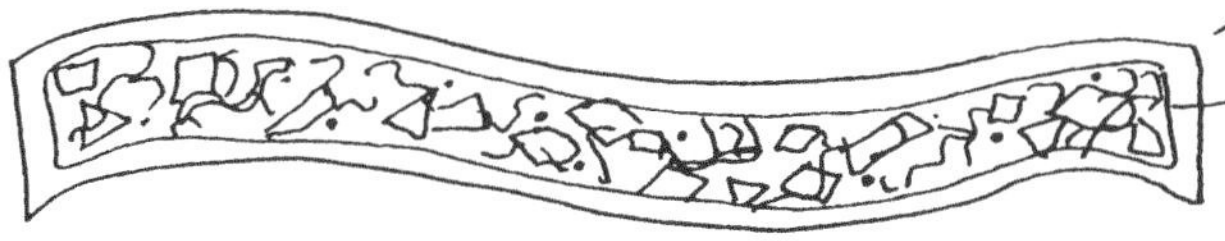

Figure 7.38

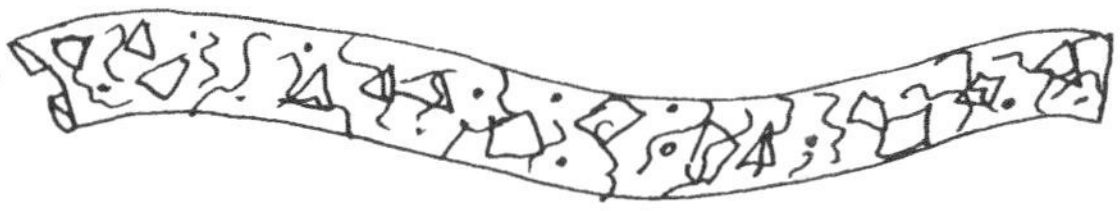

Figure 7.39

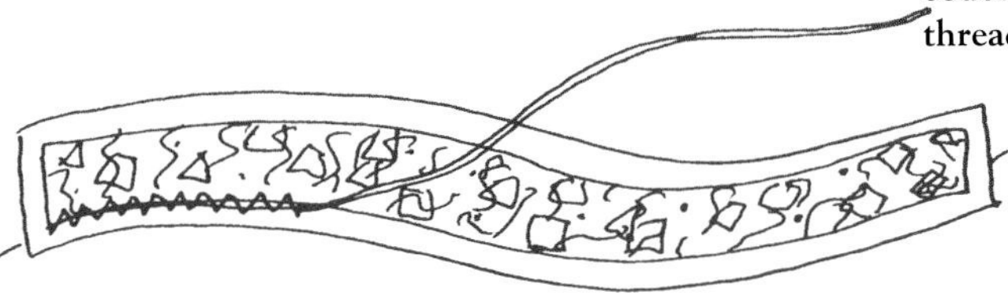

Figure 7.40

fetti cloth on the wrong side of the leather belt. Set the sewing machine for a narrow zigzag stitch. Couch the gold thread while attaching the confetti cloth to the leather belt. (See Fig. 7.40.) Just before you come to the end, stop sewing, and turn the short end of the confetti cloth under 1/4 inch. Continue couching. Repeat at the other end of the belt. Place the buckle on the belt.

3. To bead, thread the needle and knot the end of the thread. Beginning close to the buckle, take a stitch, but do not go through the leather, only the confetti cloth. Pull on the needle so the knot is pulled under the confetti cloth. Bring the needle through the confetti, add a bead, reinsert the needle, then bring the needle back up at position for the next bead. Continue working the beading across the belt. Keep a finger under the belt in the area you are working to ensure that the needle does not pierce the leather. Tie off the thread by knotting, then pulling the knot through the cloth. Finish off by taking three small stitches. Cut off the thread flush with the cloth.

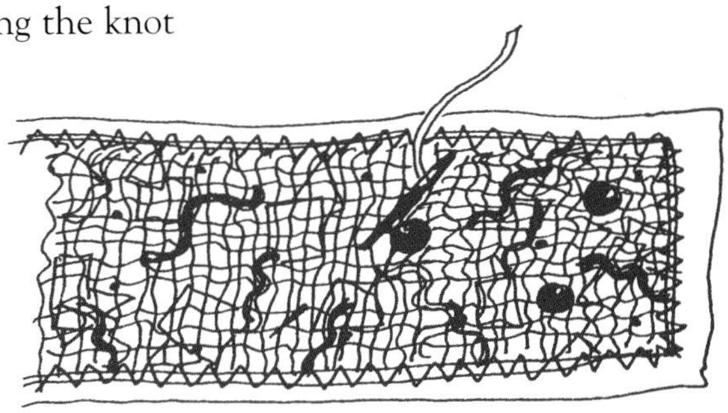

Figure 7.41

> If you are feeling artistic and inventive, buy a plain belt buckle and work a polymer clay design on it. See the polymer clay section (pages 19 to 28) for ideas.

PATTERNS

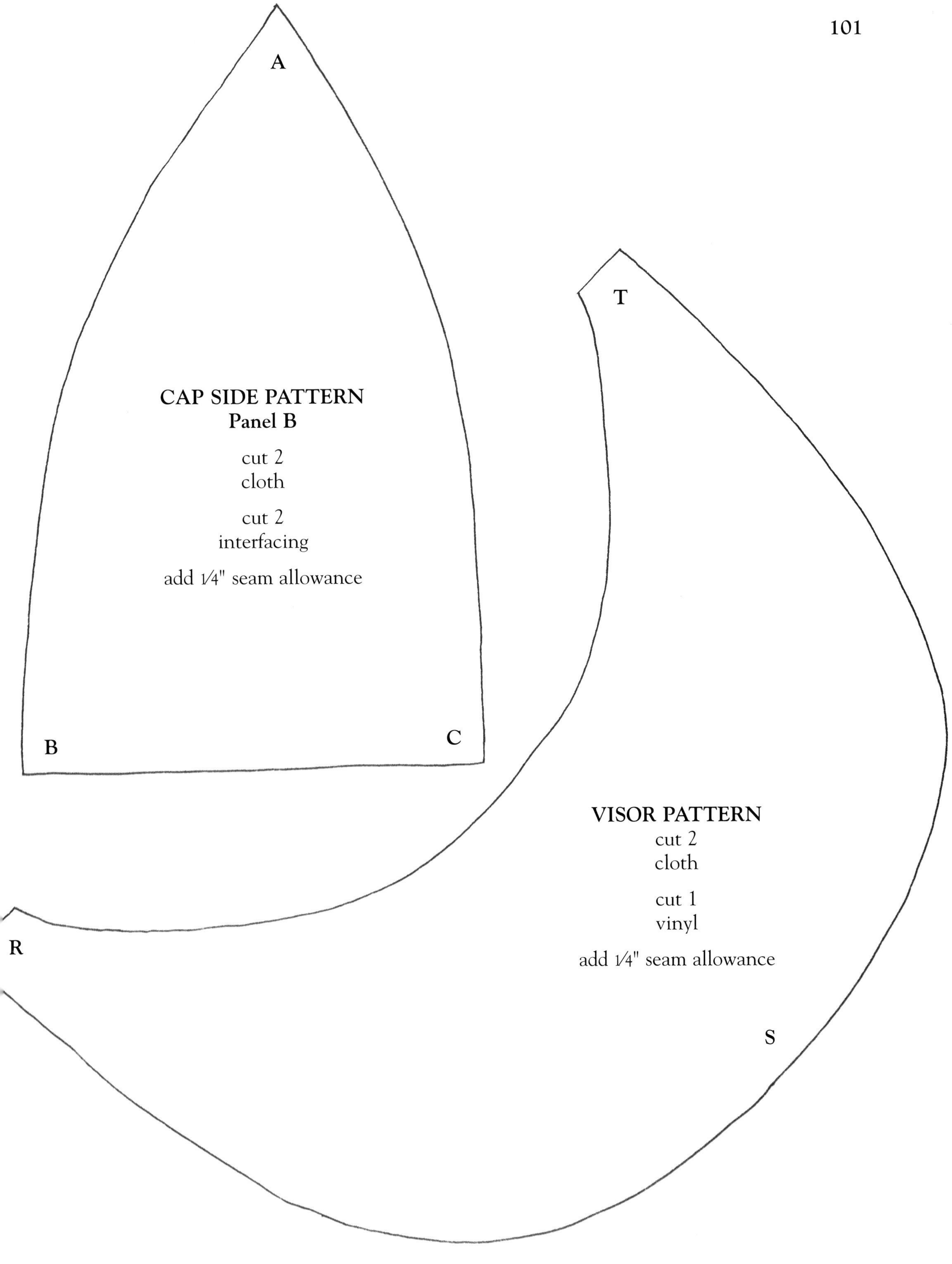
A
CAP SIDE PATTERN
Panel B
cut 2
cloth
cut 2
interfacing
add 1⁄4" seam allowance
B
C
T
VISOR PATTERN
cut 2
cloth
cut 1
vinyl
add 1⁄4" seam allowance
R
S

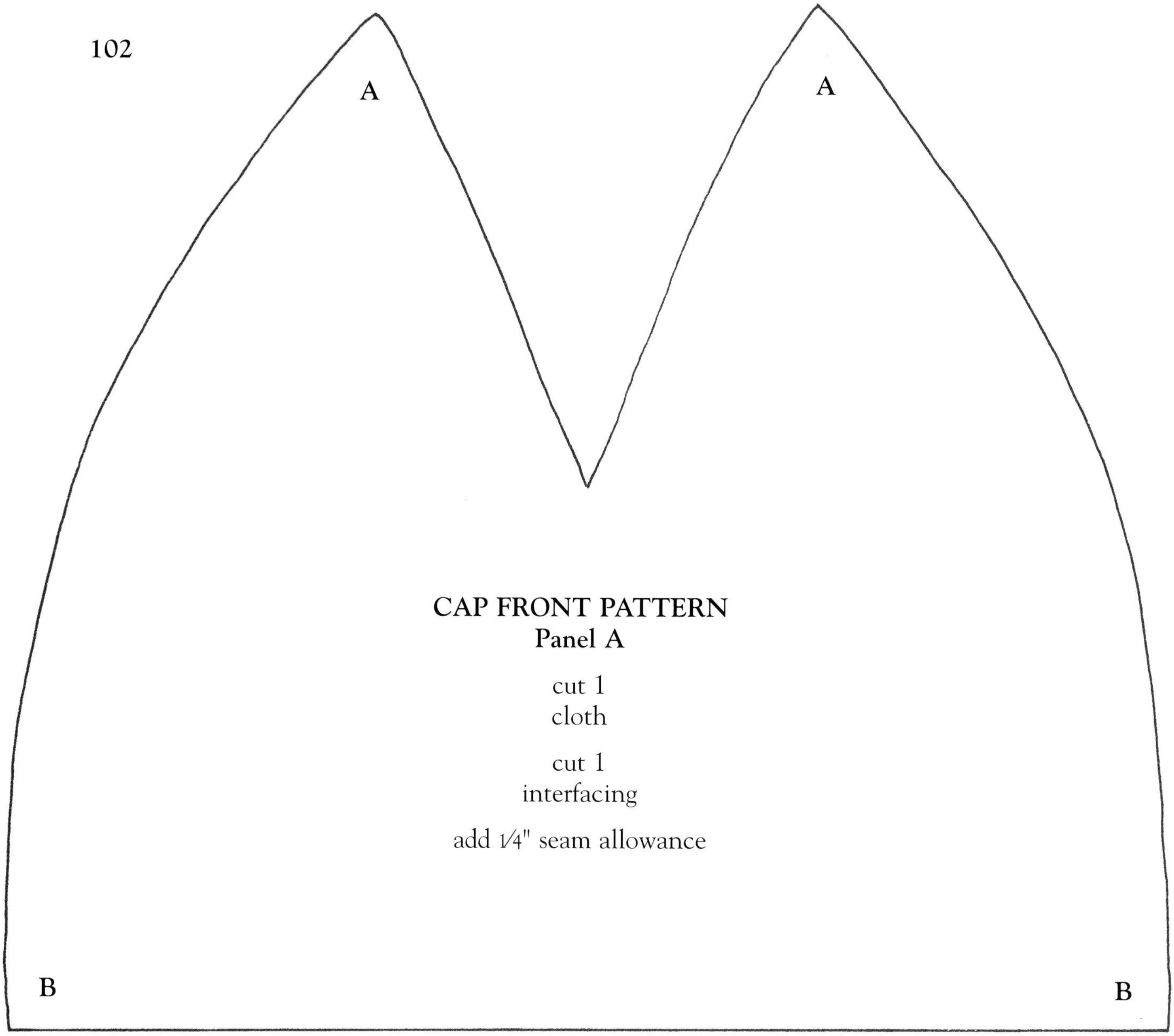
A
A
CAP FRONT PATTERN
Panel A
cut 1
cloth
cut 1
interfacing
add 1⁄4" seam allowance
B
B

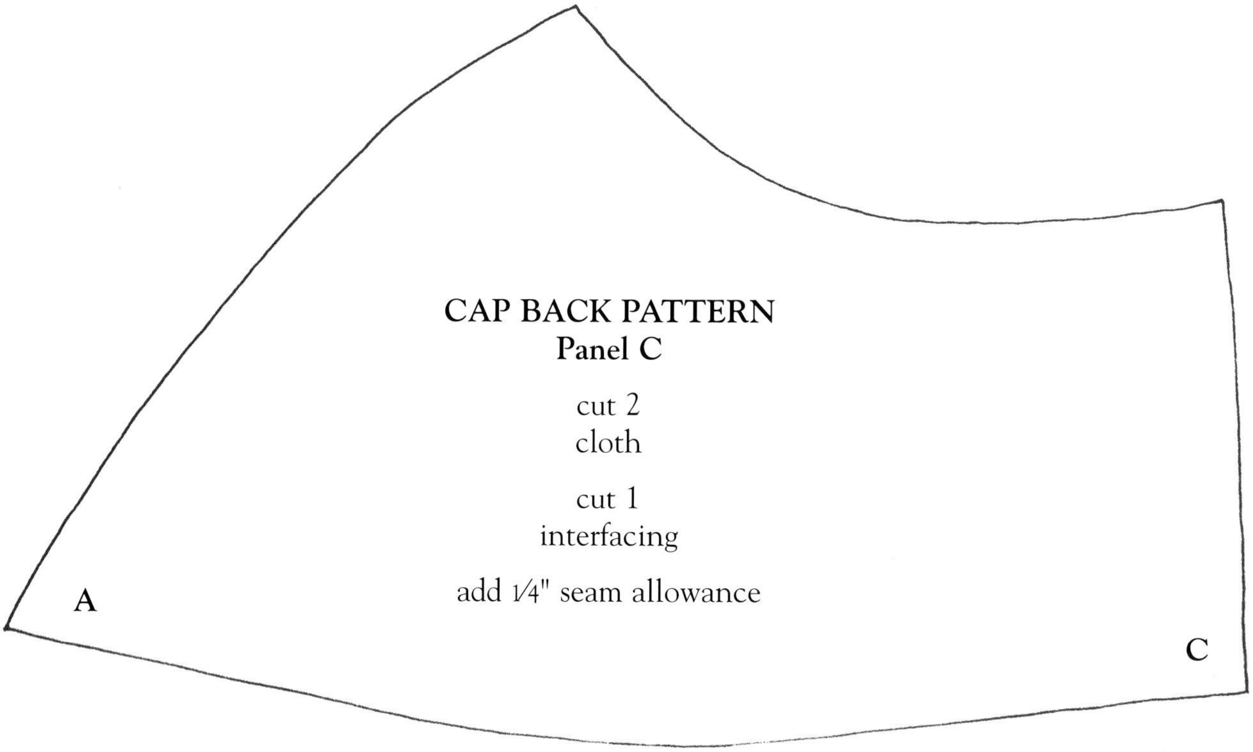
CAP BACK PATTERN
Panel C
cut 2
cloth
cut 1
interfacing
add 1⁄4" seam allowance
A
C

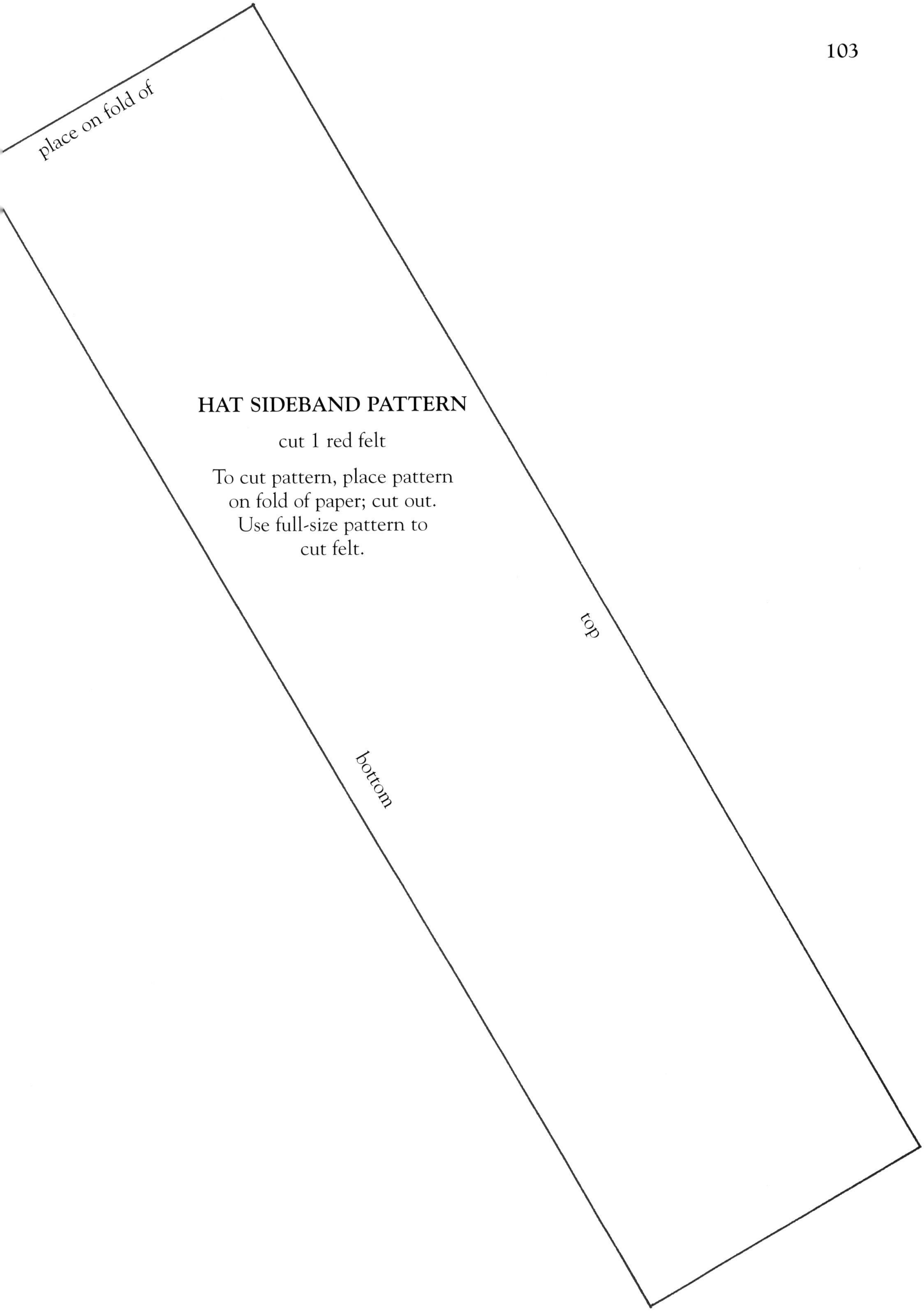

HAT SIDEBAND PATTERN

cut 1 red felt

To cut pattern, place pattern on fold of paper; cut out. Use full-size pattern to cut felt.

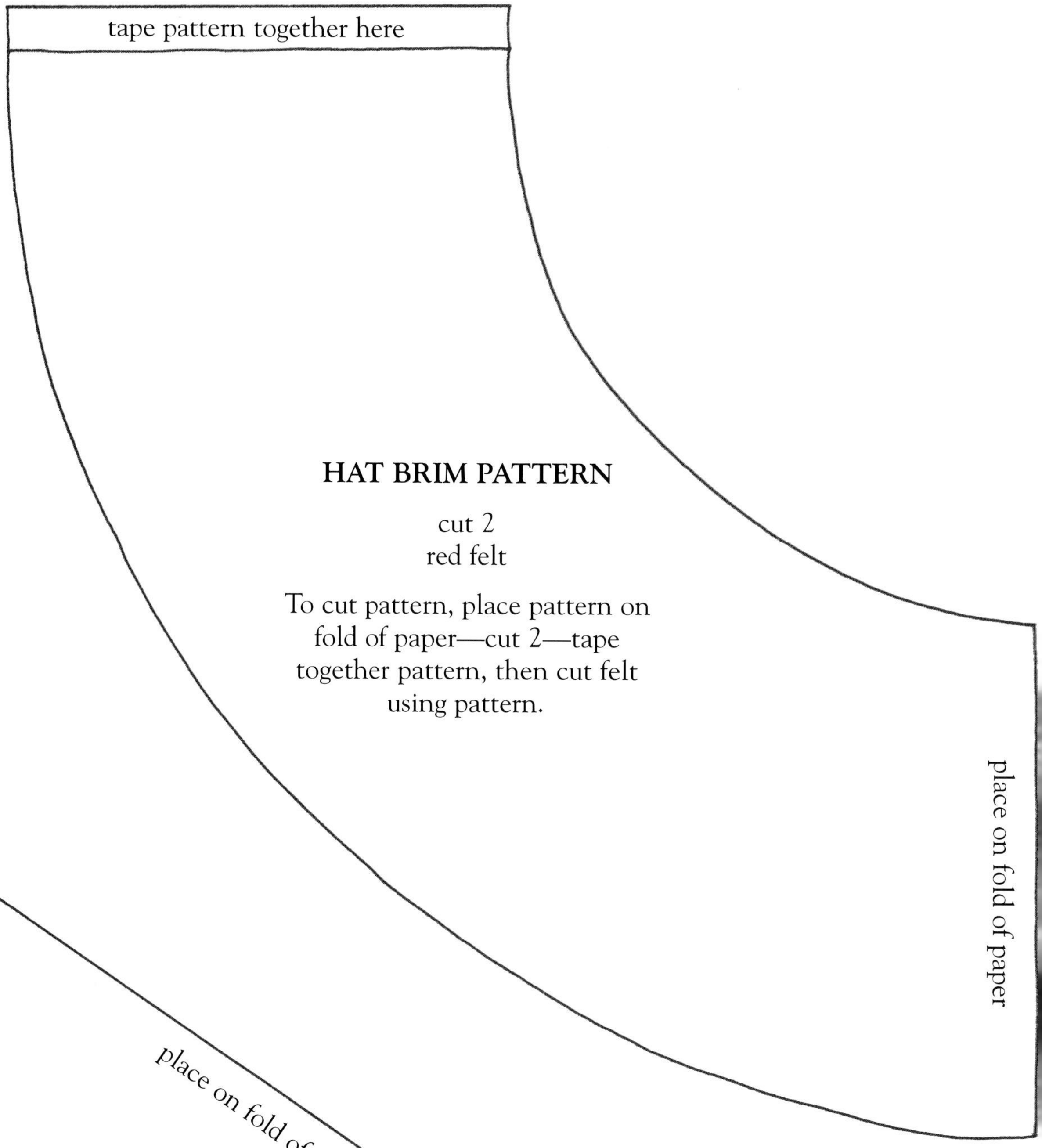
tape pattern together here
HAT BRIM PATTERN
cut 2
red felt
To cut pattern, place pattern on fold of paper—cut 2—tape together pattern, then cut felt using pattern.
place on fold of paper

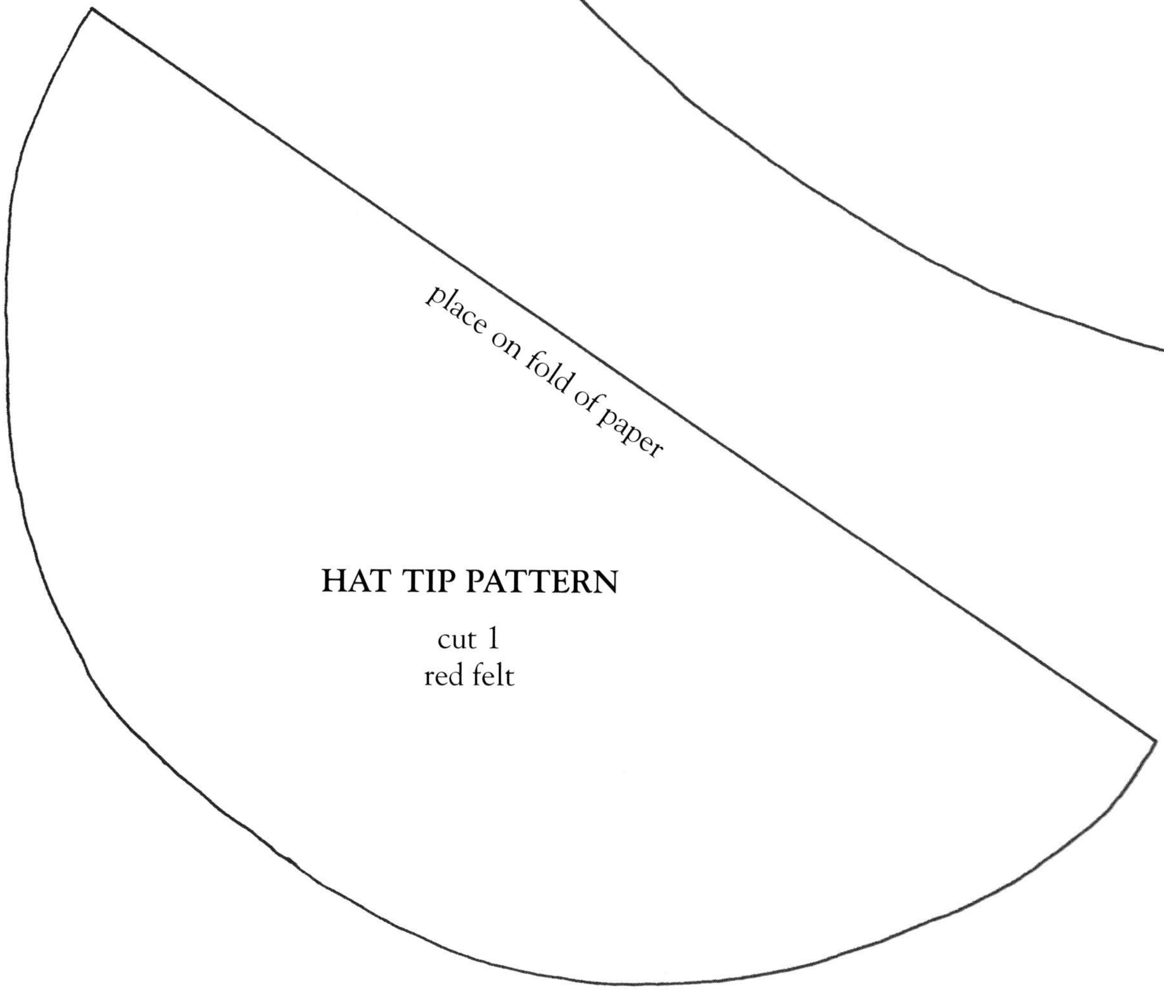
place on fold of paper
HAT TIP PATTERN
cut 1
red felt

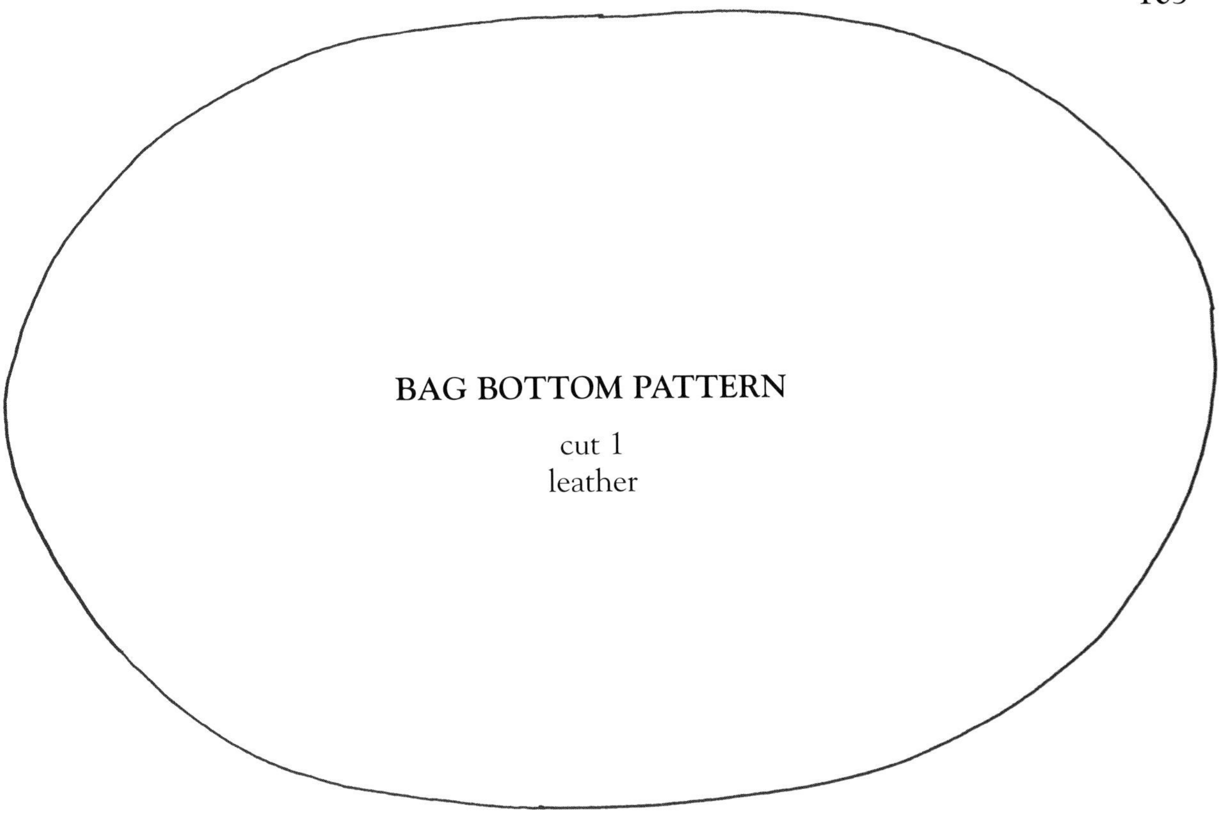

THISTLE DESIGN
PATTERN

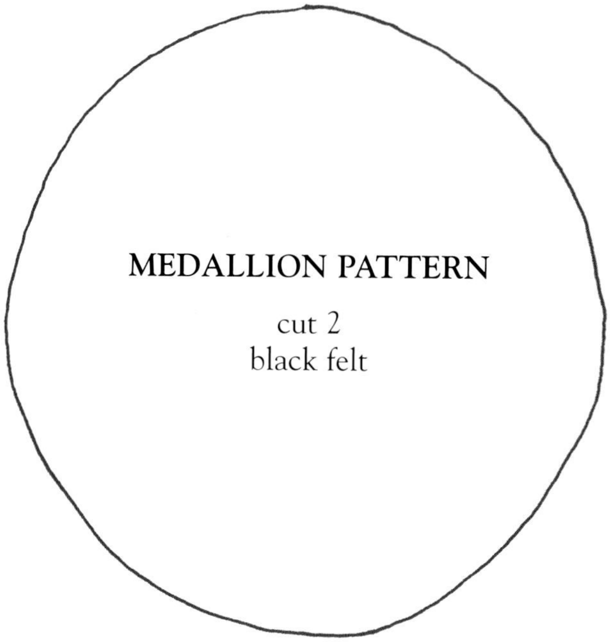

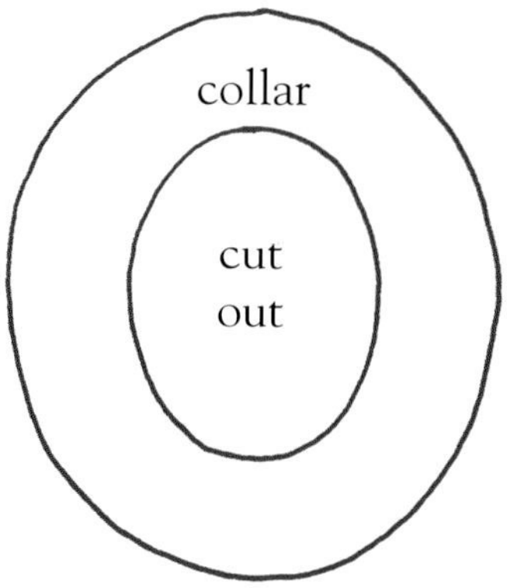

SHELL COLLAR PATTERN

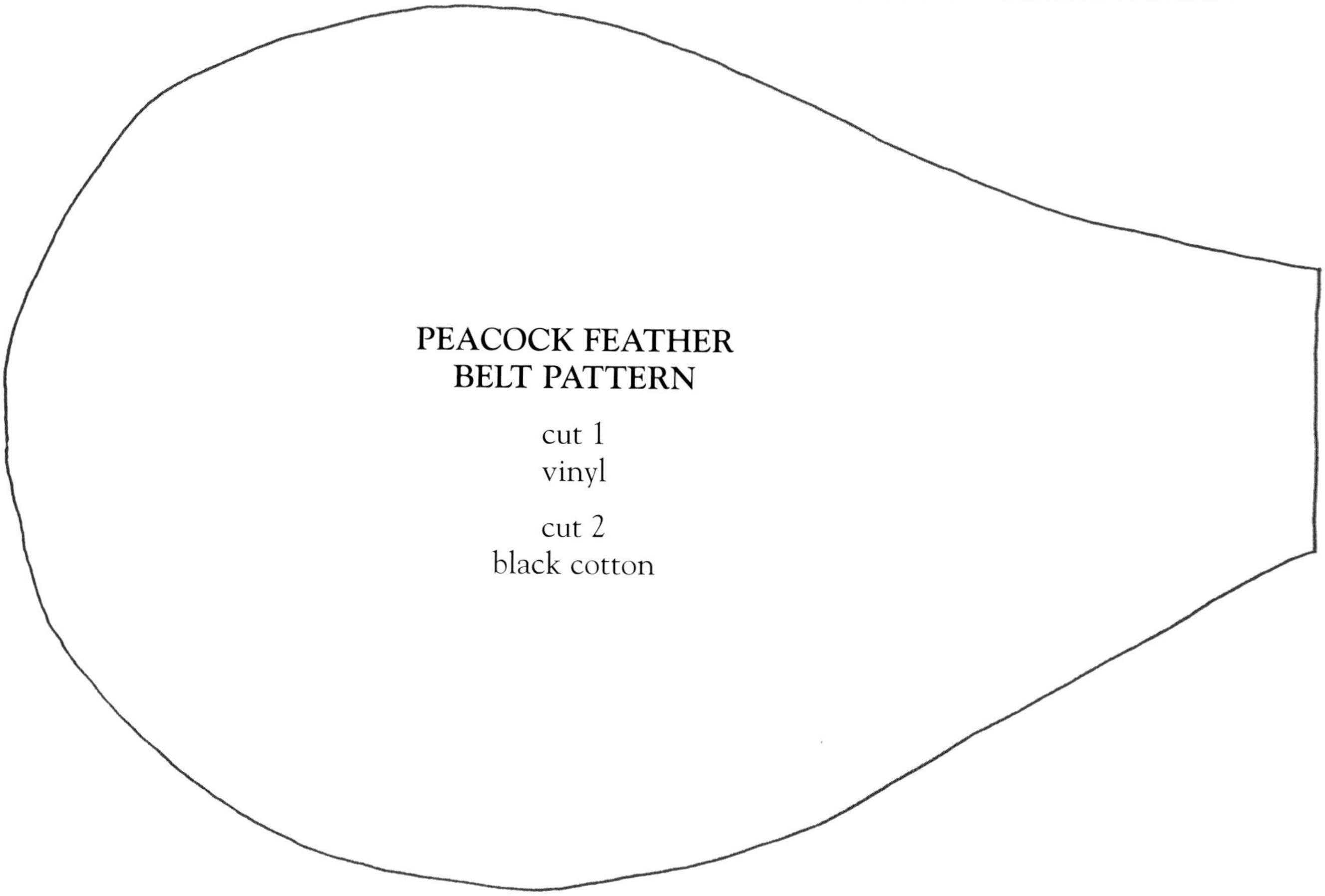

Metric Conversion Chart

The following list will help you convert measurements given in this book from inches to centimeters (or millimeters) and vice versa.

Measurements greater than ½ inch are rounded to the nearest .5 centimeter. One inch is equal to 2.54 centimeters exactly, and 1 centimeter is equal to .3937 inch.

⅛"	= 3mm	13"	= 33cm
¼"	= 6mm	14"	= 35.5cm
⅜"	= 1cm	15"	= 38cm
½"	= 1.3cm	16"	= 40.5cm
⅝"	= 1.5cm	17"	= 43cm
¾"	= 2cm	18"	= 45.5cm
1"	= 2.5cm	19"	= 48.5cm
1¼"	= 3cm	20"	= 51cm
1½"	= 4cm	21"	= 53.5cm
2"	= 5cm	22"	= 56cm
2½"	= 6.5cm	23"	= 58.5cm
3"	= 7.5cm	24"	= 61cm
3½"	= 9cm	25"	= 63.5cm
4"	= 10cm	26"	= 66cm
4½"	= 11.5cm	27"	= 68.5cm
5"	= 12.5cm	28"	= 71cm
5½"	= 14cm	29"	= 73.5cm
6"	= 15cm	30"	= 76cm
7"	= 18cm	31"	= 78.5cm
8"	= 20.5cm	32"	= 81.5cm
9"	= 23cm	33"	= 84cm
10"	= 25.5cm	34"	= 86.5cm
11"	= 28cm	35"	= 89cm
12"	= 30.5cm	36"	= 91.5cm

Guest Artists

FREYA ELLINWOOD studied with Bettina Sturm and has attended the Fashion Institute in Manhattan. She is an active member of The Bead Society of Greater New York and an officer in The New York Polymer Clay Guild. Her vision is to make beautiful, timeless statements that are appropriate for most occasions. Her pieces include beads and ornaments collected in India, West Africa, and Latin America.

DEBRA GUST credits her grandmother as the guiding light in her artistic endeavors. She holds degrees in Art and History. She first trained as a potter and weaver, then progressed to paper. Coming from a family of seamstresses, Debra uses leftover snippets of handmade paper to create the beautiful pins she has become known for. She is now exploring thermal transfers.

MYRNA KANTER is President of The New York Polymer Clay Guild and Corresponding Secretary of The Bead Society of Greater New York. Her work has appeared in *Lapidary Journal* and *Creative Clay Jewelry*. She teaches classes in polymer clay and holds a master's in Education.

BETTE M. KELLEY works in two main styles: the Egyptian broad collar and the Victorian dog collar. *Ice Storm* is an example of the dog collar style. It was inspired by a horrific ice storm that was awesome in its grandeur and breathtaking in its beauty. The main emphasis of Bette's work is three-dimensionality and intricacy. Nature is her main source of inspiration.

ROBERTA Z. MARCO studied illustration but soon began making padded posters that eventually led to making stuffed pins. She has always been interested in fashion accessories and creates hats, evening bags, dyed and embellished gloves, and jewelry, both for herself and to sell.

MAXINE PERETZ PRANGE began collecting beads with the notion she would incorporate them in her handweaving. But the beads—from lampworked glass to bone to Fimo—became necklaces. Currently, she is working in peyote stitch creating kimonos and various other shapes. Maxine feels her jewelry is suited to the woman who wants to tell the world that while she may not be flamboyant, she certainly doesn't want to just blend into the crowd.

Recommended Reading

If you'd like to learn more about creating jewelry and accessories, I'd like to suggest the following books for your reading pleasure.

Bagley, Peter, *Making Modern Jewellery*, Cassell, London, 1992.

Good design ideas. Covers fine jewelrymaking, but the ideas would easily translate to the materials used in Dazzle. *Includes an interesting leather tassel bangle, peacock feather earring, and very unusual two-color feather earrings.*

Bawden, Juliet, *The Hat Book*, Lark Books, Asheville, North Carolina, 1993.

This book is loaded with full-color step-by-step photos on how to make and embellish hats for men, women, and children. A must for the hat lover!

Bosence, Susan, *Hand Block Printing & Resist Dyeing*, David & Charles, London, 1985.

Look for this book at your local library to read about wax resists.

Creating Fashion Accessories, Singer Sewing Reference Library, Cy DeCosse, Inc., Minnetonka, Minnesota, 1993.

A roundup of clever ideas from various artisans. Lots of color step-by-step photos.

Dodson, Jackie, *How to Make Soft Jewelry*, Chilton Book Company, Radnor, Pennsylvania, 1991.

Exciting book filled with projects for making lots of appealing jewelry out of many different materials. Highly recommended!

Kennedy, Jill and Jane Varrall, *Silk Painting*, Chilton Book Company, Radnor, Pennsylvania, 1991.

A book by British authors covering everything to do with silk painting. This book includes a description of the sugar resist method.

McConnell, Sophie, *Metropolitan Jewelry*, Bulfinch Press, Boston, 1991.

A delicious array of paintings through the ages, focusing on the jewelry depicted in the art. Well-written historical information.

McCreight, Tim, *The Complete Metalsmith*, Davis Publications, Inc., Worcester, Massachusetts, 1991.

Although this book is aimed at artisans working with fine metals, it contains information of interest to artistic jewelrymakers including mokumé, bezels, clasps, etc.

Moss, Kathyrn and Alice Scherer, *The New Beadwork*, Harry N. Abrams, Inc., New York, 1992.

A gallery-type presentation of all the exciting work being done with seed beads.

Robinson, Julian, *Fashion in the 40's*, St. Martin's Press, New York, 1980.

A wonderful little book—very British in tone—covering the tailored fashions of the 1940s. Check out the hats. This is a nice motivational piece.

Roche, Nan, *The New Clay*, Flower Valley Press, Rockville, Maryland, 1991.

This is the best book available on using polymer clays. Covers technique with a nice overview of what's going on in this field.

Taylor, Jacqueline, *Painting and Embroidery on Silk*, Cassell, London, 1992.

Very thorough book on painting on silk. Good explanation of how to do special painting effects.

Tomalin, Stefany, *Beads!*, David & Charles, London, 1988.

Very succinct book covering materials, some techniques.

Resources

Suppliers

Aardvark Territorial Enterprise
P.O. Box 2449
Livermore, CA 94550
Lively newspaper/catalog of unusual items. Sample copy $2.00.

Aiko's
3347 North Clark St.
Chicago, IL 60657
Beautiful handmade papers. Catalog $1.50.

American & Efrid, Inc.
P.O. Box 507
Mount Holly, NC 28120
Signature thread—hand-quilting, metallic, rayon, 100% cotton, transparent. Available at your local sewing center.

Beada Beada
4262 North Woodward
Royal Oak, MI 48073

Bead Art
60 North Court St.
Athens, OH 45701

Bead Bazaar
1001 Harris St.
Bellingham, WA 98225

Bead Boppers
1224 Meridan E.
Puyallup, WA 98373

Beadazzled
1522 Connecticut Ave., NW
Washington, DC 20036

The Bead Fairy
178 Ramona Dr.
San Luis Obispo, CA 93405

The Bead Museum Store
140 S. Montezuma
Prescott, AZ 86303
Beading books

The Bead String
1336 Cesery Blvd.
Jackonsville, FL 32211

Beads Unique
308 Roberts Lane
Bakersfield, CA 93308

BeadZip
2316 Sarah Lane
Falls Church, VA 22043
Catalog $5.00.

Berger Specialty Co.
413 E. 8th St.
Los Angeles, CA 90014
Wholesale.

Boston Bead
3734 28th St.
Grand Rapids, MI 49512

Caldron Crafts
1520 Caton Center Dr.
Suite E
Baltimore, MD 21227

Casa de Oro, Inc.
756 Caddo St.
Corpus Christi, TX 78412

Cerulean Blue, Ltd.
P.O. Box 21168
Seattle, WA 98111-3168
Adjustable fabric frame, dye, paints, brushes.

Clay Factory of Escondido
P.O. Box 460598
Escondido, CA 92046
Polymer clay. Wholesale.

Columbine Beads
2723 Lock Haven Dr.
Ijamsville, MD 21754
Catalog $5.00.

Communication Concepts
P.O. Box 23505
Columbia, SC 29224-3505
Distributor for Palmer Paint Products (glues, glazes, and mediums) and Madeira Marketing (GlissenGloss "fantasy fibers"—Fiesta, Estaz, Frizz, and Fiesta Wire).

Crafters Choice
12 North Orchard
Boise, ID 83706

Craft Gallery
P.O. Box 145
Swampscott, MA 01907
Books and supplies.

Decart, Inc.
Lamoille Industrial Park
Box 309
Morrisville, VT 05661
Deka paint products—Deka Gloss, Deka Permanent, Deka Silk.

Delta Technical Coatings, Inc.
Whittier, CA 90601
Renaissance foil and related products.

Dharma Trading Co.
P.O. Box 150916
San Rafael, CA 94915
Thorough catalog of everything for silk painting; also, silk yardage and prehemmed scarves.

Diane's Beads
1803 West Main St.
Medford, OR 97501

Discount Bead House
P.O. Box 186
The Plains, OH 45780
$3.00 for a year's worth of catalogs (4 or 5).

Earth Guild
33 Haywood St.
Asheville, NC 28811
Dyes, polymer clays, books.

Evening Star Designs
69 College Ave.
Haverhill, MA 01832
Catalog $3.00.

The Gardin' of Beadin'
P.O. Box 1535
Redway, CA 95560

General Bead
317 National City Blvd.
National City, CA 91950

Graphic Chemical & Ink Co.
728 North Yale Ave.
Villa Park, IL 60181
Watercolor paper, brayers, mediums, etc.

Hanson's Leather
6900 Andressen Rd.
Sheridan, CA 95681

Heidi's Craft Garden
124 Hillside Ave.
Williston Park, NY 11569

International Beadtrader
3435 S. Broadway
Englewood, CO 80110
Catalog $5.00.

June Tailor, Inc.
P.O. Box 208
Richfield, WI 53706
Quilter's Cut 'n Press II (one side has a cutting mat, the other a pressing mat).

Kuma
Box 2712
Glenville, NY 12325
Beads and supplies.

Lewis C. Smith
P.O. Box 176
Medford, OR 97501
Catalog $2.00.

Loew-Cornell, Inc.
563 Chestnut Ave.
Teaneck, NJ 07666-2490
Quality paintbrushes, brush cleaner, accessories.

Manny's Millinery Supply
26 West 38th St.
New York, NY 10018
All millinery supplies.

Morning Light Emporium
P.O. Box 1155
Paonia, CO 81428

Napa Valley Art Store
1041 Lincoln Ave.
Napa, CA 94558
Art supplies, watercolor paper.

Nomad Notions
4906 North May Ave.
Oklahoma City, OK 73112

Ornamental Resources, Inc.
P.O. Box 3010
Idaho Springs, CO 80454
350-page black-&-white catalog, $15.00.

Personal FX
P.O. Box 664
Moss Beach, CA 94038
Catalog $5.00.

Polyform Products, Inc.
P.O. Box 2119
Schiller Park, IL 60176
Sculpey III polyform clay, matte and gloss glazes, tools.

Rupert, Gibbon & Spider, Inc.
P.O. Box 425
Healdsburg, CA 95448
Jacquard Silk Color Kit (includes dye, chemical fixative, applicator bottle, fine tip, bamboo brush, booklet); catalog includes everything for silk painting.

Savoir-Faire
P.O. Box 2021
Sausalito, CA 94966
Sennelier dyes for silk and wool, Tinfix all-fabric dye/ink, Peintex all-fabric color.

Shafaii Co., Inc.
1000 Broadway
Houston, TX 77012
Catalog $2.50; minimum order $50.00.

Sheperdess
2802 Juan St.
San Diego, CA 92110

Shipwreck Beads
2727 Westmoor Ct. SW
Olympia, WA 98502
Catalog $3.00; $25.00 minimum order.

A Stitch Back In Time
11026 Sagittarius Rd.
San Diego, CA 92126
Catalog $3.00.

Supplies 4 Less
13001 Las Vegas Blvd. S
Las Vegas, NV 89124
Catalog $3.50.

TSI, Inc.
101 Nickerson St.
Seattle, WA 98109

Westcroft Beadworks, Inc.
139 Washington St.
South Norwalk, CT 06854
$50 minimum order.

Yasutomu & Co.
490 Eccles Ave.
South San Francisco, CA 94080
Handmade papers.

World Beads
2640 East 3rd Ave.
Denver, CO 80206

PERIODICALS

Adornments—The Bead Journal
P.O. Box 177
Fox River Grove, IL 60021
Quarterly journal highlighting technique, history, ideas, news. $19.95 per year.

Bead & Button
P.O. Box 1020
Norwalk, CT 06856-1020
Quarterly of projects in color. Covers all types of handmade jewelry.

Lapidary Journal
Devon Office Center, Suite 201
60 Chestnut Ave.
Devon, PA 19333-1312
Emphasis on fine metal jewelry but also includes beaded jewelry. Nice to see design work.

Old Jewelry News
Jewelry Marketplace Publishing, Inc.
P.O. Box 272
Evanston, IL 60204
Quarterly newspaper of ads to buy and sell old jewelry, beads, etc. Repair services.

Ornament
Ornament, Inc.
1230 Keystone Way
Vista, CA 92083
Gorgeous four-color quarterly focusing on artistic jewelry.

I would like to take this opportunity to thank all of the manufacturers who have continually developed new and better products for artists and crafters. In the past 20 years this impressive product development has brought pleasure to everyone—from the seasoned professional to the novice using creative materials for the first time. Thanks!

About the Author

Self-portrait by the author.

LINDA FRY KENZLE is an artist/designer well known for her striking use of color and unusual techniques. Linda's award-winning work has been shown nationally and internationally. During the 1980s Linda published *Stylepages*, an inspiring sewing journal.

Linda is the author of six books, including the best-seller *Embellishments* (Chilton, 1993). Currently she is writing two new books, *Casual Chic* and *Adornments*.

In her leisure time, Linda enjoys gardening (specializing in propagation and plant history), reading, bicycling, and swimming. She is also taking flying lessons from her brother Charlie.

Linda lives along the banks of the Fox River in northern Illinois.

For lecture and workshop information, write:

Linda Fry Kenzle
P.O. Box 177
Fox River Grove, IL 60021